To the only female I love, res
more tha

This book is dedicated

"In Nature, nothing hurries. Yet all is accomplished."

To David

Merry Xmas, mate!

December 2014

Foreword

During early 2013, I kept seeing little snippets passed about on Facebook attributed to an ancient Chinese philosopher called Lao Tzu. Many of them seemed to relate directly to some of the mental challenges I was facing in both my work and my personal life. After a search, I finally discovered a user friendly translation of Lao Tzu's work, '*Tao Te Ching*' and sat down to read it. What had really drawn me in was the concept within this philosophy of a generic, inexplicable natural order. In my own scribbling's ... hundreds of magazine articles, wildlife blogs and two books ...I have always tried to impart my belief in the natural presence that I have always referred to as 'Mother Nature'. The more I studied the '*Tao Te Ching*', the more I realised that the folk who developed this manuscript (written two and half millennium ago) were in tune with Nature and the natural order in exactly the same Way that I have been while sitting quietly in the woods and fields of my beloved Norfolk, watching the behaviour of bird, beast, wind, water, sun and moon. Yet, though I recognised so much of my own thinking within the 'Tao Te Ching' it also raised a few conflicts which my troubled my spirit. Like many philosophies that evolve into *'religions'*, there is an undercurrent of the *'Tao Te Ching'* being the only 'Way'. I have always understood that the human psyche often needs a *'Way'*, a doctrine, an ideal, an understanding to cling to. If only to make sense of the roller-coaster ride that is life, birth, death, health, disease, glory, failure, celebration and tragedy. I'm no different. My personal ideology has long revolved around my 'Mother Nature' and my temple, the place where I go to reflect and to heal ... is the countryside. If I take issue with any of Lao Tzu's writings it would be around the occasional reference to the 'Valley Way', which I assume to be the pastoral, passive lifestyle of the Chinese ancients. There are, throughout the *'Tao Te Ching'* some condemnations of sport, hunting and arms. Far from annoyance, I found mild amusement in this. Particularly as the Chinese were such a martial people when it was written.

I am a countryman and Hunter. Because of this, I understand the ways of bird and beast better than many. My craft depends on observation and knowledge. When I move quietly through the forest, I am in tune with the forest. I am part of the ecology, part of the food chain, part of the *'circle of life'*. One of Lao Tzu's 'ten thousand things'. I am an animal and my presence there is as natural as that of the owl, the buzzard, the deer, the crow or the squirrel. My right to act in the interest of crop, stock or songbird protection ... or to hunt to eat ... is surely as inherent to Natural law as is the stalk of the hungry fox or the stoop of the falcon? All of this made me re-visit the *'Tao Te Ching'*, several times. It is not a long work, by any means ... but it is a profound work. Too meaningful to dismiss or to cast aside simply because you don't believe or understand all that is written within. We need to understand that this work has scripted the Way of life for millions of followers for so, so long ... and in my humble opinion, quite rightly so. There is much 'life advice' in the *'Tao Te Ching'*.

Rather than dismiss it, I chose a different path (a different Way) and set out to take each chapter and interpret it in a Way to which I could relate. The following chapters, therefore, are not a direct translation of the original Chinese text. Neither are they intended to offend the practising Taoist. Nor (despite my use of the masculine throughout) is it intended to infer sexism. I know many countrywomen and female hunters who put their male counterparts to shame. I refer to Nature throughout as a *'she'* ... for she definitely is. No male could be so beautiful yet so equally benevolent and harsh. Thus it made sense to call the Hunter, *'he'*, simply to avoid confusion.

This, The Hunter's Way, is intended as a tribute to the principles of the *'Tao Te Ching'* that can be understood by the woodsman, the stalker, the naturalist, the shooter, the forager, the farmer, the ranger, the game-keeper, the pest controller ... in fact anyone who finds solace, sustenance or even employment in the countryside. To those who may find this work 'sacrilegious', I offer this simple thought. The original Way, the *'Tao Te Ching'*, advises the reader not to bear arms. Yes, I bear arms in my hunting. It also advises the reader to spurn righteousness. So put down your crucifixes, your beads, your incense burners and your secularism ... and I will gladly lay aside my tools too. The *'Tao Te Ching'* was clearly written as philosophical advice, not as the basis for a creed. I am passionate in my pursuit of knowledge and wisdom about the immediate natural world that surrounds me. I'm not faintly interested in the false two-dimensional world of the television documentary, which influences (biases) so many minds. The conservation of rare species and the balance of natural eco-systems are part of the true woodsman's remit. I believe myself to be a good, ethical Hunter. The Hunter's Way is intended to simply pass on some advice (as I do with all my books) on the values which make the ethical Hunter more than simply a wildlife assassin. For (believe me) I encounter plenty of them.

For every verse of the *'Tao Te Ching'* I re-interpret here, there is also an explanation of what it means to me (and hopefully, you) as you go about your hunting. If you aren't a Hunter and pick up this work, I hope it will go some Way to explaining the psyche and purpose of those of us who choose the path of Hunter / conservationist.

Be happy. Be honest. Most of all ... be wild.

Ian Barnett
April 2014

One

Nature is the name we give the life force pulsing all around us.
Beyond Her is the supreme mystery which created Nature.
What lies beyond Nature is incomprehensible. Some call it the Way.
Nature is the mother of a billion things.
She manifests herself in the wonder of the wild world.
Without striving we can see the tapestry that Nature weaves.
We may never see the reason for the weaving. Nor does it matter.
It is a privilege to see it and accept it for what it is.
Some will be satisfied to simply enjoy the weave and the weft.
Others will study and observe, seeking to understand.
The Hunter will understand more than most, yet never all.
No-one, though, will ever explain the Way. Nor does it matter.
Enjoy the enigma. Not knowing is part of the awe.

For thousands of years, Mankind has sought explanation for the wonders that surround us which can't be explained. Even in this modern era of scientific study and the plethora of '... ology's' seeking to find understanding and source, we still have the unexplained. Early civilisations, without such insight, built myths and gods and doctrines around all this mystery. Many of these still exist. It is not my intention to challenge any of these here. What interests me more is the common view of Nature, as a miracle of life (and death); a rich cycle of renewal and decline; an intangible force responsible for the existence of not just all living things but also their environment. All doctrines also seem to agree that Nature is but the offspring of some deeper, more powerful entity. The real mystery. Some call it the Tao (meaning the Path), some call it God. It matters not what we call it. It fills the space between every particle, living or inert. It ebbs and flows. It fills and empties. It is beyond good or evil; beyond light or dark; beyond dead or alive; beyond right or wrong. It simply 'is' and those who find it claim they are 'enlightened'.

Two

Nature's balance displays beauty and decay in equal measure.
She shows benevolence and cruelty in equal measure.
What is good for some of Her charges is bad for others.
What is bad for some of Her charges is good for others.
The gale-felled tree shelters the ground game and hides the vulnerable.
The leaf fall feeds the soil to grow and sustain the next tree.
The wind disguises the vixens stalk and the rabbit falls prey.
The zephyr exposes the foxes musk and the rabbit lives.
The long summer day allows Her charges to forage and feast.
The bitter winters chill presses them to merely survive.
This years diseased rabbit warren bears no fruit.
Next years warren is fertile and abundant.
The sun rises, the sun sinks. The moon waxes, the moon wains.
The tide flows, the tide ebbs. Seasons rise, seasons fall.
The Hunter watches and adjusts to Nature's conditions.
He takes when it's right to take and leaves when it's wrong.
He adds where he can and expects no credit.
He sustains what is important and protects what is vulnerable.
So that it is there tomorrow. So that it is there forever.

Though many of us will never find that enlightenment, we can all find Nature for it surrounds us. Yet few truly do. I mean real Nature, not false Nature. I don't mean a walk through the blue-bells or a trip to the zoo. I don't mean staring at a television documentary or reading a glossy wildlife magazine. To really find Nature you need to go into the wild and watch it in all its glory or its modesty. To understand Nature, you need to understand life and death, growth or decline, health or disease, compassion and cruelty. Most importantly you need to understand man-kinds role in Nature. We are a participant in this eternal drama, not the author of it. That honour falls to a much more reliable entity. Nature herself. As one of the higher organisms in Her design ... and one of the alpha predators ... we can influence that drama but should never seek to control it. The Hunter, who spends much of his time steeped in the study of the wild world around him, is in a position to respect Natures work. To see first-hand what Nature is capable of. To benefit or to suffer at Natures hand. The human Hunter is just another predator in Natures design yet has the benefit of not just reasoning but conscience. No other wild predator has the latter. For that reason alone, the Hunter must exhibit control, restraint, compassion and respect at all times. He must learn to conserve and to farm, not to slaughter. To protect the vulnerable species, thus helping maintain Natures balance, yet never annihilating other species. This is what I call The Hunter's Way.

Three

Go modestly about your business, never bragging.
Braggarts attract attention and dislike.
Hunt silently and gracefully, like the barn owl.
Don't seek to accumulate prestige through hunting..
Prestige provokes jealousy and challenge.
Never display your catch or your weapons openly.
Then people cannot criticise your purpose or methods.
The wise Hunter goes humbly through life.
Feeding and nurturing his charges, preserving and farming.
The competent Hunter should counsel modesty, not power.
Lead by example, discouraging cruelty and greed.
If your own charges are content with this, you can do no more.

Mankind has many legitimate and morally defensible reasons for hunting. Gathering meat for the pot, gleaning hides and pelts for clothing, protecting livestock or vulnerable species being among them. Many hunters, myself included, can find no ethical excuse for trophy hunting. The death of a wild creature at a hunters hand should be untainted by bragging or gloating. The Hunter who takes delight in the execution of a creature is no countryman. This is not to say that delight in the execution of a clean dispatch is wrong. The latter is what should please the Hunter. Efficiency, mercy and compassion, not death. There are many examples in the predator chain that the Hunter should emulate. The barn owl is one of my favourites. Silent, modest, economic in movement and selective in its hunting. It takes enough to survive, no more. It sits for ages watching the landscape then strikes accurately and mercifully fast. It doesn't willingly display its catch, often taking it away to feast. A model Hunter.

Four

Nature is infinite. She has no shape or substance.
She cannot be emptied, nor can she be filled.
Yet Her intangibility creates a billion tangibles.
She provides shelter against Her own keen wind.
She draws the cloud curtain to shade the scorching sun.
She drenches the arid fields and woods with rain.
She unleashes the sun and wind to dry the drenched earth.
She ties Her knots, throwing challenge to Her charges.
She unties Her own knots, through the wonder of evolution.
She makes the lowest wondrous, the highest humble.
That which she moulds from the earth, she returns to the earth.
She is unfathomable but always at work.
We know not from whence she sprang.
Only that she is as ancient as time itself.

The Hunter spends many waking hours in the study, the pursuit of understanding, of Nature and Her charges. This is an endless, never accomplished endeavour. To really appreciate Nature you must empathise with Nature and all Her wonders. Yet you must understand that to simply watch, perhaps record and to be part of this wonder is all we may ever achieve. If you accept that we may never fully understand why Nature can be so contradictory, so fickle, so beautiful in one moment yet so ugly the next ... you might retain your sanity. We are merely one species of the many under Her charge. We have our role to play in life's rich pageant, yet no claim to exclusion from Her changing mood or purpose. Nature gives and she takes away. Never always, it sometimes seems, in equal measure. In Her grander scheme, there is undoubtedly balance. Nothing lies wasted when she unleashes Her own raw fury. Even the fallen creature or tree feeds the carrion feeder, the maggot, the worm, the beetle or the mycelium. Take the latter, the creeping microbe which feeds on decay then blooms as the fungi, to spread its spores on the wind to assist Natures cleansing team elsewhere in the wood or field. Magic.

Five

Nature is neutral. She is incapable of bias.
She treats Her billion charges with equity.
The Hunter should be equally impartial.
He should treat his charges with equity too.
Nature's cadence is in a constant state of flux.
She expands and retracts. She is there, yet appears not to be.
She takes control and she relinquishes control.
She lifts and she drops. She pushes and she pulls.
The Hunter should behave like Nature.
His actions should mirror his equanimity.
He must achieve balance, give and take in equal measure.

Imagine Nature as being like the reflection of a swan in calm lake. She is there but she is not there. You can't grasp Her yet you can clearly see Her. Cast a stone into the pool and the ripples will disturb the image momentarily but it soon restores itself. That is Natures cadence. Self-levelling, self-repairing. Like the swan, Nature appears calm and beautiful but beneath the surface there is motion, propulsion and purpose. The efficient Hunter should act like this. Calm and serene, yet focused and determined. Reflection has an important part to play in the Hunters Way. The yin and the yang. life versus death, light and dark, good versus evil, balance over bias. The Hunter should consider action versus consequence ... or inaction and outcome. Most importantly, the Hunter must remember the creed of the fruitful farmer. He must put in to take out. He must protect and nurture his environment, respecting every living thing. Control but never eradicate.

Six

The spirit of Nature drifts between the trees unseen.
Across the field and hedge, over the mountain, through the vale.
She kisses the top of the rolling ocean wave.
She dives into it's depths to spread Her influence.
She is constant and secure, like a mother.
Her roots are deep within the earth, Her breath above the clouds.
The Hunter knows she is there but will never see Her.
He will see only the fruits of Her unseen labour.
He will trust Her implicitly, for she always prospers.
No matter how long it takes, she always succeeds.

Walk through the frosted wood in the depths of winter beneath grey, skeletal boughs reaching to a gunmetal grey sky. Where now the bud and the leaf? Try to touch the misted breath you exhale. Walk out onto the sown barley field. Feel beneath your boots the granite-hard ground that entraps a million tiny seeds and wonder how they can possibly survive under such hoary captivity? Note the ewe huddling for shelter against the dry-stone wall, a bundle of pregnant fleece, the barrier between the keen Arctic blow and the foetus she bears within. Walk the same wood in a few months, humming to the orchestra of insect life and the murmur of doves, green and verdant. Walk to the margin of the field to watch the tall barley stalks billowing like a soft ocean, stirred by a warm breeze. Watch the lambs frolic. Nature always succeeds. Never, ever doubt Her.

Seven

The sky above your cap endures forever.
And the earth below your boot endures forever.
Why is that? How can they endure forever?
Because they were never birthed, never spawned, never sprouted.
They don't exist for themselves. They don't feed, drink, reproduce, die.
Therefore they exist forever. They are the platform and the space.
Platform and space for Nature's constantly changing tapestry.
The more the Hunter can accept this, the wiser he will become.
The more he detaches from himself and becomes one with Nature.
The more he will understand and achieve unity with wild things.
The Hunter needs to feel part of the spirit of wood and field.
Only then will he feel fulfilment within Nature.
We are not permanent like the sky and the earth.
There was no before. There will be no after.
We will return to the Way, as do the other billion things.
Thus fulfilment is in the 'now'. Not in the past or in future.

The earth, the oceans, the rivers, the lakes and the sky are the infrastructure on which ... and within which ... life not only exists but also travels. Therefore they are superior within the Way, as the living organism. Without them, no life would exist. If they are essential to life, then they are part of Nature, above the billion things. The Hunter must understand this and respect that this infrastructure is as crucial to his existence and livelihood as the blood that courses through his veins. The Hunter, privileged to walk in wild places and watch wild events, recognises more than many folk how low we are in the fabric of the Way. Yet the Hunter also knows how high we are in the hierarchy of Natures billion things. Consider this? Because Nature can only exist within the atmosphere that envelopes the earth, Nature is as tethered to the earth as Her charges. Surely it is better to have proven value within Natures design than to seek suppositional immortality within the Way. Ask yourself two simple questions. Which will endure longer? The cathedral ... or the mountain? The temple ... or the ocean? Mankind's inclination to seek immortality through religion insults Nature. So many lives wasted in pursuit of redemption or in seeking sanctity and piety, when the real purity of life is in actually living it. To the full, now.

Eight

Virtue and integrity are like water.
Water sustains Nature's billion charges.
Nothing can survive without its touch.
Even in the most meagre trickle.
Water exists where man and beast cannot.
Water flows and penetrates, un-resisted,
Therefore water is, like Nature, everywhere.
Virtue needs to be like water. Everywhere.
In life, in living, stay close to Nature and the earth.
In your thinking, penetrate deeply, like water.
In contact with others, be virtuous, be like water.
Flowing and invigorating. Honest. True.
Like Nature, to your own charges, be neutral.
In your work, prove your competence.
Always think before you act.
And only act when appropriate.
Then no-one can contend your action.

Water, life's most essential element, often behaves like Nature and often behaves like Natures creator, the Way. It swirls between crack and crevice. It dissipates throughout the landscape, sometimes passively, sometimes violently. Yet never mistake water for Nature. Water cannot be resisted but it can be diverted. Nature can never be opposed. Water moves from high to low. It can't flow upwards. Nature can. Water carves canyons and erodes earth and rock to force it's path to the open sea. Water often displays its supreme power ... the tempest, the flood, the torrent, the tsunami. What a magnificent element. What a superb replica of both Nature and the Way. Sometimes gentle, cool, sustaining, nurturing, refreshing, protecting. Sometimes violent, raging, uncompromising, destructive. The Hunter, in fact mankind itself, will always be lower in Natures design than water. It is not one of the billion things. It is higher than that. The Hunter, though, should try to behave like water. Go only where you can make quiet progress. Trickle slowly ... resist torrent. Look for the path of least resistance. Flow between tree and shrub. Slip over bank or dune or rock. Be fluid. Yet persist. Force the path, if needs must, to reach where you need to be. Yet do it subtly. This wisdom is life advice, not simply hunting advice. Remember that only Nature and the Way can flow upwards. If water can't, why do some men think they are higher than water?

Nine

The virtuous Hunter takes what is needed, and no more.
Stop short, even when abundance is possible. Reject greed.
Any of Nature's charges that take more than needed?
They too are designated as vermin. In need of control.
Mankind isn't exempt from this, under Natural law.
The sharpest blade soon blunts if over-used.
The gun-powder runs dry when it is needed in earnest.
Gather too much harvest and it will sit and rot, unused.
Brag of your success or your wealth at your peril.
For you will invite jealousy and plunder.
Accept that what you have achieved is sufficient.
Rejoice in your success and retire from the field, gracefully.
That is how Nature works. Achieving, inconspicuously.

Many species are labelled vermin by mankind and therefore targeted for control, often by the Hunter, though controlling pests is not hunting. Their reputation for plunder, destruction, spreading disease and wanton killing are the traits that sign the pest species death warrant. The pigeons and corvids that flock to the newly drilled plough to decimate seed and shoots before the crop gains hold. The rats that raid the grain stores after reaping, spraying the rich harvest with leptospira and fouling all that they touch. The mink that still pull the trout onto the bank, even when glutted, to take one bite then leave the fish to rot. The fox that steals into the chicken coop to behead the entire terrified flock ... then take just one on which to feed. All these are reviled. Think then how it reflects on the Hunter to abuse his status or his capability? Only hunt as much as you can carry, collect, use for food or use to feed others. Barter and sale of edible species is justifiable. Wanton killing and discarding carcasses into ditch or dyke because the Hunter has no use for them will affront Nature. The man becomes the pest.

Ten

Marry your body and spirit to Nature.
And she will never divorce you.
Open your mind to what Nature teaches.
Absorb the learning like an eager child.
Open your mind until you view everything.
As clearly as Nature sees everything.
Respect your charges and guide them.
Teach honesty and integrity, decry deception.
Embed Nature's spirit in all that you create.
Nurture Nature's spirit in all that you do.
Let Nature's wisdom counsel your thoughts and actions.
Nourish and mould without claiming possession.
Offer help without expecting reward.
Lead without dominating. Achieve without arrogance.
This is how Nature displays Her virtue.

The Hunter, spending time in the wilderness amid either the tranquillity or the chaos that is Nature, appreciates its purity. He will learn far more from these encounters and this exposure than can be written in any book or shown on any screen. Sound and vision need to be supplemented with scent, touch and taste for anything we humans experiences to be 'real'. In the wild, in Natures huge agenda, nothing happens or exists without purpose. Understand this and you soon learn to evaluate the intent and purpose of the existence of every living thing, including Mankind. You will soon learn that compared to Natures honest design, our own is hugely flawed. We are an arrogant species, claiming to know Nature better than she knows herself. Attempting to change or distort Her design for our own purpose. The Hunter, the farmer, the shepherd, the countryman ... those who truly know and live with Nature ... work with Her. Never against Her. They teach acquiescence with Nature. They trust Her fickleness and temperament implicitly. The red sky at night? They know its portent. The halo over the rising sun? They know its meaning. The rook throng labouring low over the fields and back to the roost? The Hunter and all his country friends will be heading for cover too.

Eleven

The hole at the hub of the cartwheel.
Is what makes the wheel useful.
The empty space with-in the cook-pot.
Is what makes the pot a vessel.
Doors and windows cut into the walls.
Are what change a room from a cell to a living space.
It is the hollow void within the rifles barrel.
That allows it to serve its purpose.
The empty circle of air with-in the snare.
Is what allows it to catch and fill the larder.
A footprint in the mud or snow is nothing but empty space.
Yet its value is enormous to the Hunter.
The Hunter may well profit from what is 'there'.
Yet often, it's what is 'not there' that is useful.
The wise Hunter understands this.

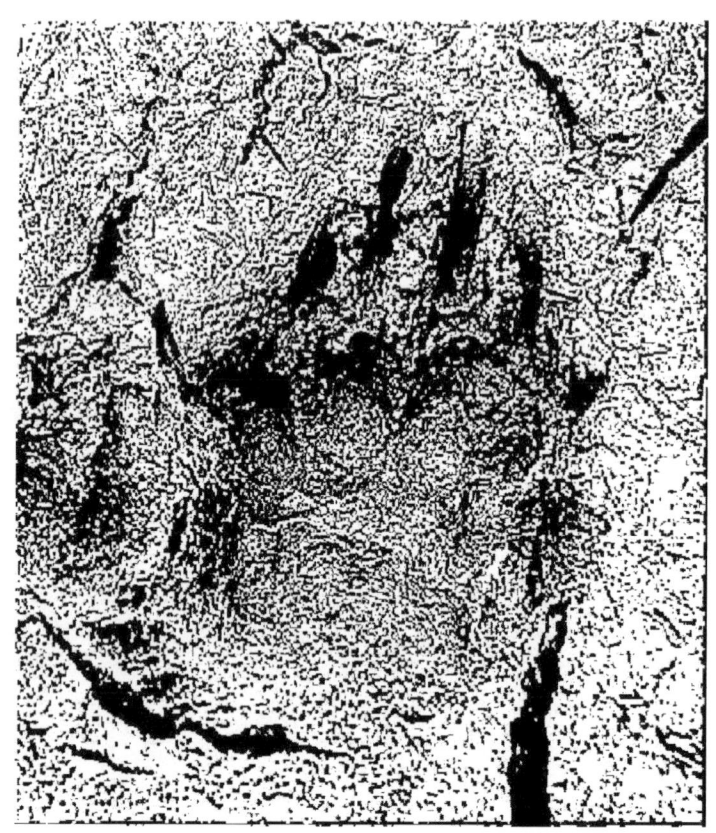

The Hunter will see many manifestations of this basic 'yin and yang' principle as he goes about his craft. The Way is full of wise contradiction. The empty being just as important as the full. Nonentity being as crucial to Natures design as entity. No wave can roll unless the waters peak is pushed along by an empty trough. One is tangible, the other is invisible. Both working in harmony to achieve a purpose and move an ocean. The thrushes nest is of no use without the empty cavity in which to lay Her eggs. This deep 'yin, yang' essence is not just about emptiness and fullness. It spreads throughout Nature in many guises. The Hunter must learn its significance and its logic. The unearthly silence before the violent storm tells the Hunter the first thunder-bolt is imminent. During a gale, the pattern of the wind is like the ocean swell. Gust, then calm. Yang, the masculine ... then yin, the feminine. The Hunter can read this pattern and still stalk effectively. The gusts cover the sound of movement while the calm, the empty space, allows the shot. The Hunter will always need a knife. When he sharpens the blade it is the removal of steel that makes its edge keen. Thus, just as the Way explains, the Hunter profits not from what is there ... but what is not there.

Twelve

The colours of the rainbow blind the Hunter's eyes.
The Hunter should use Nature's colours, plain, simple.
Excess noise deafens the ear of bird, beast and man.
The wise Hunter moves, speaks and acts silently, always.
They say mixing five flavours destroys the taste of a dish.
So the Hunter should relish the single flavour.
He should harvest the abundant. Never the exotic or the rare.
He should focus on one quarry but be ready react to others.
He should avoid the chase. Instead, stalk slowly.
Seeking what you cannot catch will drive you insane.
He should let go of what he cannot sensibly attain.
Concentrate on what he can realistically achieve.
Achieve what comes naturally to his purpose and demeanour.
The rook doesn't try to feed under the full moon.
Nor does the red squirrel try to fish for brown trout.
Follow your head, not your heart. As wild things do.

In my own writing I have always advocate that simplicity is what makes the Hunter successful. Try to use the same gun for as many purposes as possible so that you come to know it intimately. There is an old saying 'Beware the man with one gun, for he knows how to use it'. It is true and based an old Oriental martial arts adage which said similar. 'Fear not the man who knows ten thousand kicks, fear the man who has practised one kick ten thousand times'. The Hunter should know his limitations and work within them. The over-stretched shot is futile. Using insufficient power is futile. Using too much power is futile. Hunting should be about balance, poise, pragmatism and assessment of each situation. Natures natural canvas is muted in colour, rustic. So the Hunter should blend in to this. His actions should mimic his wild counterparts. Watch the roe deer traverse the wood and I challenge you to hear its footstep. Study the vixen as she squats near the rabbit warren, sitting licking Her lips. Unless the conies get nearer, she will not move. A chase over open ground won't serve Her purpose for she knows she will lose the race. Cunning and stealth win the prize, not impatience. The Hunter must learn this. Sometimes it is better to concede defeat. A single missed shot at a young quarry species will educate it enough that you may never get a second chance.

Thirteen

Success and failure are equally challenging.
Yet not as challenging as our perception of ourselves.
Success makes you confident, yet sometimes reckless.
Failure erodes confidence. It breeds dereliction and despair.
Why do I say self-perception is challenging?
Because success can go to your head, failure can discourage you.
Step back from your achievements or disappointments.
Reflect on them. Understand what went or wrong.
Why do I say self-perception is challenging?
The little owl hunts infrequently and watches for long periods.
Yet the little owl never goes hungry. She is usually successful.
Why do I say self-perception is challenging?
Because to fail is natural yet Nature never fails.
What you used to think of as 'failure', was not.
It was simply what Nature intended. Learn from it. Move on.
The fox will only succeed on few of its silent stalks.
Yet the fox rarely dies of starvation. Learn from this.
Think of yourself as part of Nature and Nature will sustain you.
Be comfortable with Nature and Nature will trust you.

One of the basic principles of the Way is acceptance. Nature is flawless, so can never be wrong. Whatever happens is what is intended, cannot be changed and therefore has a purpose in Natures design. The Hunter needs to learn to accept success as reward by Nature and to understand that this privilege should never be abused. The skills he attains in his art are gifted by Nature. His quarry and the food on his table is supplied by Nature. What Nature gives, she can also take away. Equally the Hunter needs to reflect that the miss, the escape, the flight should be met with a shrug of the shoulder. It has happened. He can't turn back the clock and try again. He simply needs to do better next time. Folk who live a life dwelling on the perceived failures and disappointments of the past lose focus on the present and waste their lives in self-sympathy and regret. They risk depression and will alienate those around them who choose positivity. The circle of misery closes in on them. Folk who gain too much success often look too far forward, greedy in the pursuit of more success, more wealth, more acclaim. They risk anxiety, constantly worrying that they are not achieving enough. They miss the beauty of the present. Looking to the horizon, they overlook the butterfly at their feet or the scent of the honeysuckle at their side. Life passes them by even as it happens. The wise live in the present, where the past matters no more and the future may never occur. Thus they sit like the little owl on Her post, recognising Her opportunity when it comes. Thus they move forward like the fox, watching the fleeing pheasant without an ounce of regret.

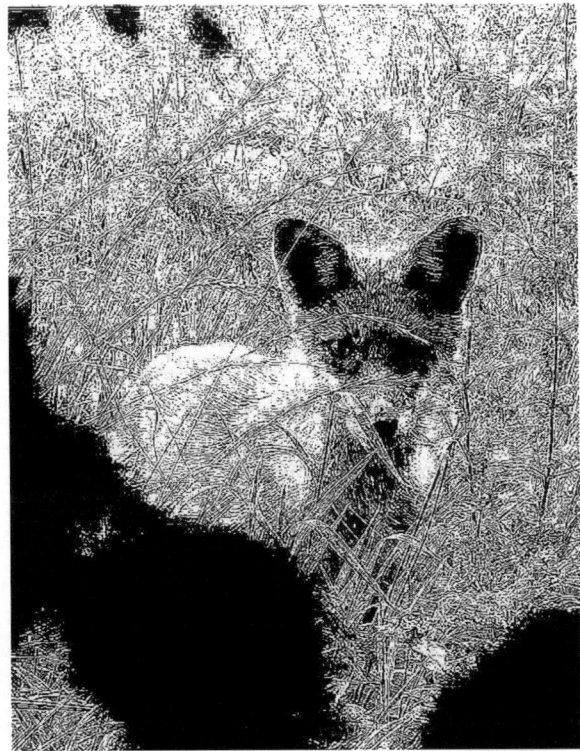

Fourteen

Though we look for Her, she is invisible.
Though we listen for Her, she makes no sound.
Though we reach for Her, she is intangible.
The essence of Nature is indefinable.
She is beyond our comprehension.
She is not found in light or in darkness.
She ebbs and flows. From nowhere, to everywhere.
From everywhere, to nowhere. Constant. Infinite.
She has no form, no face, no beginning, no end.
Respect Her. Trust she is there. Believe she is there.
Use that belief to understand the 'now'.
Rely on it, to embrace the 'now'.
Nature, the mother, was sent to balance the 'now'.
She doesn't dwell on past, nor does the future concern Her.
Embrace Nature and you embrace the Way.

The Hunter is privileged to enjoy both the hugeness and the microcosmic in Natures design. He sees the circle of life in its fullness. He witnesses the intricate building of the wrens nest, guards its progress, peeps in at the tiny eggs, keeps the magpie at bay and tries to lure the stoat from the fledglings. He watches the fox catch the squirrel that stole the egg of the jay that buried the acorn that sprouted the sapling that nourished the rabbit that fed the vixen that birthed the fox. The Hunter perceives the interaction between many species and watches its wonder. The Hunter understands Natures rhythm, Her cycles, Her portents, Her potency and Her balance. The sapling becomes the mature tree that blossoms and fruits, casting its berry to the floor, covering it in fertile leaf mulch to feed the seeds that birth the next hundred saplings. The Hunter, watching these things, knows man-kinds place in this spectacle holds no special privilege. There is no heaven, no hell, no nirvana, no Valhalla, no eternity. There is only life, gifted by the Way and only temporary. To reject this gift in pursuit of the promise of eternal existence is wasteful and arrogant. We came from Nature and we will return to Nature, having left our modest mark. Just like the seed and the sapling and the tree and the leaf mould.

Fifteen

The wise Hunter is profound and responsive.
His depth of knowledge is unfathomable.
So, being unfathomable, how do you recognise the Hunter?
He moves cautiously, as though crossing a frozen lake.
He is as heedful as a man with enemies on four sides.
He respects his environment like a visiting guest.
He blends into cover like ice melting into water.
He is stoic, like a sculptured timber.
He is open and deep, like a hollow cave.
He is opaque, like a murky pond.
The Hunter is patient enough to allow the murk to clear.
Patient enough to remain still until action is needed.
Clarity, not fulfilment, decides his course of action.

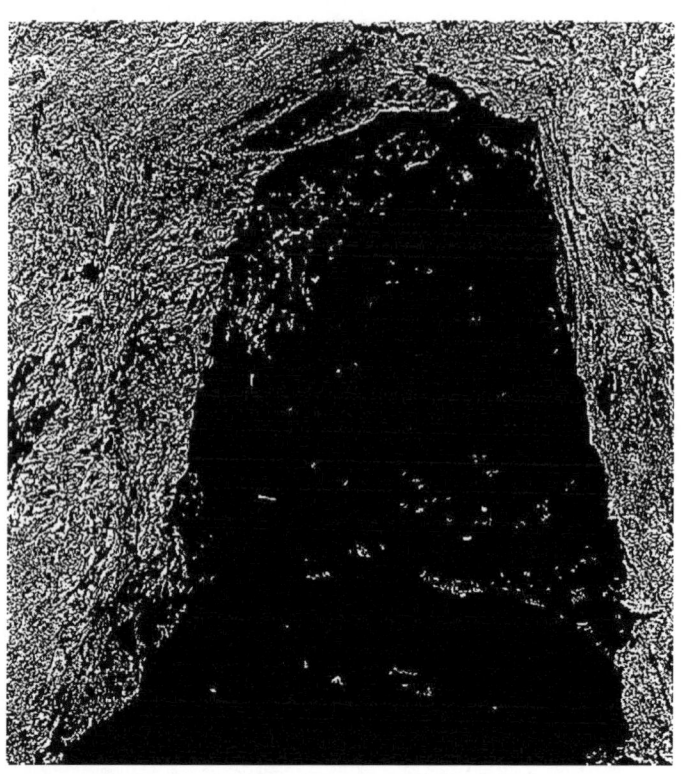

The Hunter, accepting his modest place within Natures order, should treat his surroundings and his charges with respect. When the Hunter is abroad, the landscape should be the same when he leaves, as when he entered. The gate that was shut will still be shut. The overhung branch will still hang. The soft tussock of grass under his boot will spring back. The jenny wren will sit tight on Her nest. The Hunter moves with the shadow. He is aware of all that happens around him. He stops when creatures move. When he stops, he is statuesque. He is immobile, unrecognisable, barely breathing. His mind is focused. Dark, deep, determined. He moves again only when the signs show he remains un-noticed. He is capable of long periods of patient waiting … listening and watching. He raises his gun or his bow only when he has clear purpose, full vision and complete confidence of humane despatch. He will kill swiftly, silently and with as little disturbance to the countryside as possible. He works not for the gratification of killing but for the efficient accomplishment of his purpose within this natural order.

Sixteen

Learn how to empty the mind of worldly concepts.
Sit quietly and watch Nature's billion charges.
Watch them flourish and fade. Watch the ebb and flow.
From the earth to the sky and back to the earth again.
Everything grows. Everything dies. Whatever. However.
That is Nature's Way. She is constant. Reliable in this.
Understanding this reliability enlightens the Hunter.
Those who cannot accept this constancy become troubled.
Accept Nature's constancy and you become impartial.
Life is as Natural as death. Death as Natural as life.
Nature is unbiased, therefore the Hunter must be.
The Hunter, at one with Nature, represents Nature.
He accepts the basic principle of the Way.
All the billion charges live and die. Yet Nature is perpetual.

If Nature is able to give life or deal death for good purpose, then surely so can Her charges? The Hunter is one of Nature's charges and his skills, gifted by Nature and crafted under Her scrutiny, make him Her agent in many matters. The protection of the vulnerable, the feeding of his family and the defence of his crops. The hunters key attribute is his impartiality. To be able to deal death as easily as to give life, without bias yet without troubled conscience, is a unique gift indeed. The Hunter can detach his mind from all mortal perceptions of right or wrong in delivery of natural design and integrity. He will neither celebrate nor grieve his actions. Just as his wild brethren have no concept of conscience, nor should the Hunter. The crows will plunder the crop and the songbird nest to survive and feed their young. The fox will pluck the sitting pheasant hen from Her nest to gorge. The grey squirrel will raid the chaffinch nest or strip the bark from the sapling. Many living things in Nature kill without conscience. The caterpillar eats the verdant leaf. The robin plucks the juicy caterpillar for its young. The hungry weasel steals in to eats the robin's chicks. Life covenants death to sustain life.

Seventeen

The supreme Hunter is one whose presence is unknown.
Like the fox, he passes through the wood like a wraith.
The next best is one who is respected and lauded.
He hunts like the falcon, efficient and deadly.
Below that is the Hunter who is feared and avoided.
He hunts like the stoat, wearing down his quarry.
The lowest is the Hunter who is reviled for his cruelty.
Ruthless, like the magpie, the chick-stealer.
The good Hunter trusts his charges and his students.
They, in return, will trust and respect their mentor.
He guides others and shows them how to work within Nature.
When his students say "We did that!" the Hunter has succeeded.

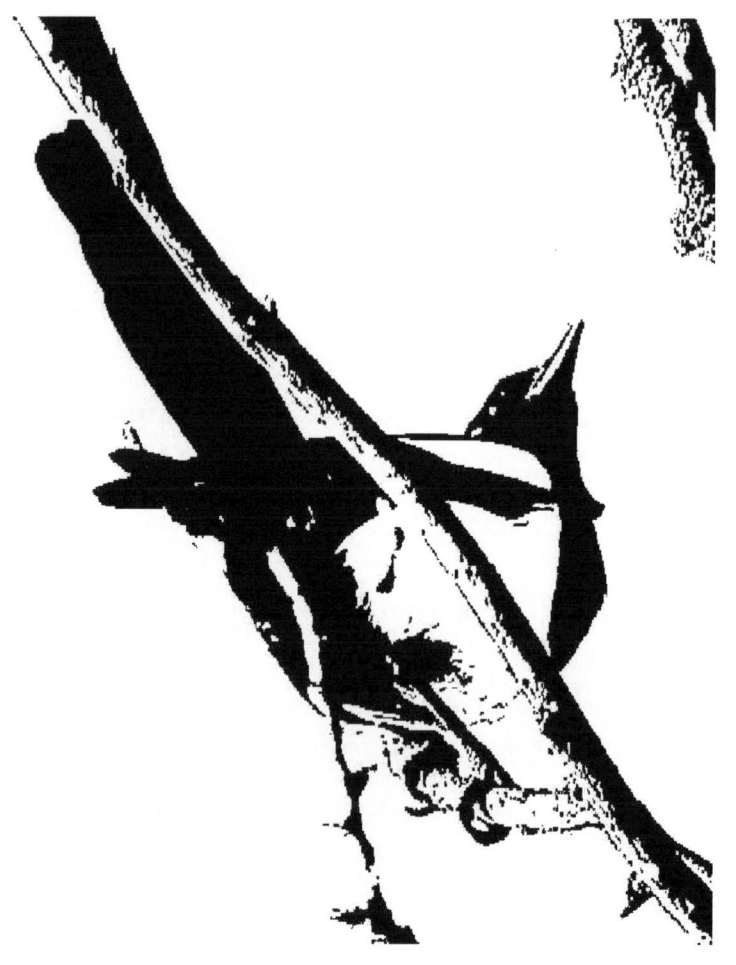

Stalker, sniper, harrier or thief? Which are you? Fox, falcon, stoat or magpie? Which are you? The fox uses silence, stealth, vigilance and cunning to hunt down prey. The falcon drops from high or swoops between the trees to strike its quarry. The stoat tracks a scent-line and follows it ruthlessly, relentlessly, until it corners its victim. In the eyes of the Hunter, magpie is a thief, a cowardly nest burglar who steals the egg or snatches the pink and helpless fledgling. In the eyes of Nature, who designed the magpie, it has purpose. Which type of 'hunting' is right, which is wrong? Many country folk despise the magpie for its habits. Rightly, they loathe the cruel human Hunter or poacher. Yet many country folk also despise the fox for its reputation for needless slaughter. Not all hunters are cruel. Not all foxes exhibit a bloodlust. The Hunter should be like the honest vixen, who kills through necessity ... with cunning and efficiency. With silence and with stealth. Without fuss. Then teaches Her cubs to do the same.

Eighteen

When people disregard the laws of Nature.
False morality and un-natural laws are created.
Politics and deception over-ride the common good.
People wrongly think that human laws are wiser than Nature's laws.
When Natural harmony is not taught, it is not inherited.
Children lose touch with Nature. They believe what they are told.
Nature's enlightening and constancy is lost.
Those who preach dis-harmony are joined by others.
Ignorance prevails and the worm is mistaken for the snake.
Predators enjoy protection while the passive are slain.
Mankind has a role to play in restoring balance.
The Hunter and the conservationist dance the same dance.
Though the tunes to which they dance may often differ.

We are surrounded by the well-meaning but misinformed as we go about our business in the countryside. One of the sad by-products of increasing urbanisation is that humans are losing touch with Natures order. The circle of life. The deerstalker is frowned upon while the abattoir is conveniently forgotten as the populace scan the supermarket shelves. The angler is criticised while the city child thinks their fish-fingers fell from the sky. The walker in the town park wonders where the robins went, as grey squirrels frolic at his feet. The sanctity of life is taught to the young with no explanation that often it is death that begets life. The Hunter who chases the fox is maligned, accused of cruelty. Yet the fox, that slaughtered the twenty hens and only ate one, is a poor persecuted thing? Nature favours man and his methods over the fox, just as she favours the fox and his methods over the hens. That is Natures order. Conservation and hunting go hand in hand. If the vulnerable deserve protection then the children should be taught that we have an important part to play in that protection. For Nature has deigned it so.

Nineteen

Ignore religion, dogma and secular teaching.
If all mankind did, we would benefit immensely.
Nature is about life and living, not death and afterlife.
Resist modern notions of charity and morality.
People need to recover Natural feelings and emotions.
Re-discover Nature, discard materialism.
Then the frauds and thieves will disappear.
Yet, these are all just outward adjustments.
It is more important to adjust the inner-self.
Respect the pure, see simplicity and ignore ego.
Let go of ambition. Nature doesn't recognise ambition.

So many lives are wasted in pursuit of sanctity and purification. Searching for immortality is man-kinds biggest vanity. Who are we to seek a higher place than the ant or the eagle? So many wars fought, so much conflict and atrocity inflicted on often innocent people under the banner of 'religion'. Nature doesn't recognise religion or creed or dogma. Watch Her when she rages. She doesn't throw forth the tsunami and leave all of one creed alive, the others drowned? Do they all go to the same heaven, nirvana, Valhalla to live for eternity? The Hunter should be like the deer or the falcon. Live life to the full, within Nature, with no certainty except death. That Way, you will absorb every moment and enjoy every breath. Be honest and be respectful yet ensure that you live without obligation to un-natural law or false agenda. Aspire to life, not to sainthood. Nature does not elevate any living thing to such ridiculous arrogance.

Twenty

No-one should worry that their Way is right or it is wrong..
Who decides what is wrong and what is right?
One person's good is another's bad.
One mans weed is another man's wild flower.
Why should we fear what others fear?
Nature is detached, limitless and immaterial.
Many folk find recreation in material things.
Many folk look for Nature but fail to see Her.
The Hunter, drifting with Nature, is part of Her.
He watches and learns, like a new born cub.
Many covet wealth while the Hunter expects little.
Who is the fool? They will say 'the Hunter ' is.
They believe that they are clever, the Hunter simple.
They think they are studious, the Hunter obtuse.
Yet the Hunter is deep and tranquil, like a calm sea.
The Hunter is as powerful and as free as the winter gale.
He is like the crow. Vigilant, intelligent, deft and parochial.
Others bustle, searching for goals and achievement.
The Hunter stands apart from yearning, fulfilled instead by Nature.

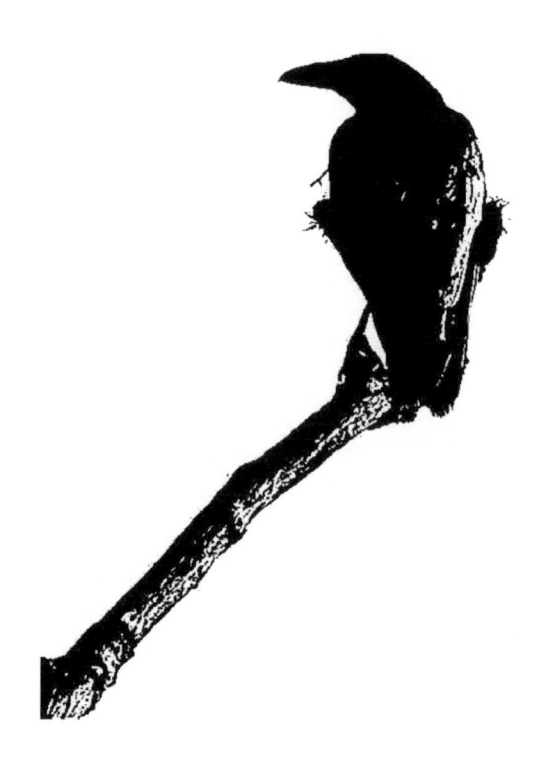

The Hunter need not fear what others think of him or his lifestyle. Nature allows his behaviour and what Nature condones can never be wrong. He is merely different in his existence than other men. He seeks fulfilment through being at one with the wild and spending time in the wilderness. He will look upon and admire the beauty of a flush of honey fungus as many folk would look upon a Rembrandt or Picasso. He will watch the flight of the greylag skein with the same wonder as many men will watch the passing of a beautiful woman. He will appreciate the sound of the booming bittern amongst the reeds as some will thrill at the roar of rally car engines on the start-line. Many folk will look at the Hunter, his plain clothing, his scuffed boots, his tattered cap and his dirty truck thinking 'here is a simple man with simple means'. How wrong they will be. What they see is someone who holds no value on the disposable or shallow accumulation of material possession. Someone who takes satisfaction in humility, not vanity. The Hunter has a deep, analytical, perceptive mind. The Hunter is all-knowing yet ever-learning. He listens ... to hear all; looks ... to see all; scents ... to smell all; touches ... to feel all. He is as fit and powerful as Nature needs him to be. Not for him the needless search for wealth and material possession. Not for him the climb up the corporate ladder or the need for status and empowerment. The Hunter walks the field and wood with no agenda other than to be part of the environment, accepted within Nature. Fulfilled by sight and sound and scent and touch ... and most importantly, purpose.

Twenty One

To believe in and to trust in Nature.
That is the greatest path to follow.
How can you follow what is intangible, elusive?
How can you follow enigma and ambiguity?
Watch the subtle power in the sprouting seed.
See the pure simplicity of the songbirds egg.
Witness the transition of caterpillar to butterfly.
Enjoy the emergence of everything, from nothing.
These are real. Tangible. The essence of life.
Miracles of Nature, performed since the advent of time.
To appreciate the enigma, you must be part of the enigma.

The Hunter knows that the Spring that follows the Winter, which follows the Autumn, after the Summer is a perpetual cycle. Nature's cycle. It can be trusted and relied upon. The building of nests, the laying of eggs, the casting of a winter coat for summers, the casting of antlers for velvet of new growth, the moult of feathers, the migration of bird species. These are as regular and reliable as the mist of the hunters frosted breath or the beating of his heart. The barley seed that breaks the previously hoar-hardened soil. The burst of the fragile dandelion head to disperse a thousand seeds. The tiny rabbit kits cowering beside the burrow as they first see daylight. All of these trivial miracles which demonstrate the total consistency of Nature. The Hunter relies on these cycles and he knows them intimately. He is part of the miracle, part of Nature herself. Otherwise, she would never show him such things. He is, invited by Nature, part of Her mystery.

Twenty Two

Sometimes you must yield in order to overcome.
Sometimes only bending will set you straight.
Empty the heart and head and they can be re-filled.
Work to exhaustion and rest until replenished.
If you possess little, you can receive much.
Those who gather too much, cannot profit from more.
The wise Hunter embraces Nature's guidance.
Performing his work modestly, he excels.
Never needing to justify himself, he accomplishes.
Never boasting, he receives high praise.
Never bragging he cannot, therefore, fail.
Never challenging others, he remains unchallenged.
The wise say 'yield and you will overcome'.
Precious wisdom, born in Nature.
Act with equity, like Nature, and all will come your Way.

Nature constantly demonstrates the principle of passiveness standing firm in the face of fury. The slender reed and the teasel stand aloft under pressure from the gale and the downpour. They survive because they are pliant and flexible, therefore able to bend with the gust and beneath the deluge. All folk need to recognise when they are tired or over-worked. Rest is simply bending to the storm. It is healthy and wise, not a weakness. The Hunter should take enough to feed or to satisfy his employer. He should never take excess, nor desire the over-flowing cup. What cannot be used is waste and the Hunter must avoid waste, as does Nature. Economy, efficiency, modesty and achievement are all that are required of the Hunter. He should resist conceit and avoid contest. He who is better is not necessarily best. A self-proclaimed champion is often surrounded by challengers. The true 'sensei', the real master of his craft, works skilfully and humbly, never seeking fame. Those who matter know his proficiency and that is enough for him. He feels no need to display his success and so no-one seeks to usurp his reputation. He acts like Nature and achieves the wonderful without claiming credit for it. Nature, she who expects and respects humility, rewards it with accomplishment.

Twenty Three

Nature does not announce Her intentions. That is not Her Way.
The raging gale will only endure for hours.
The heavy deluge is swift, but passes.
What dictates this? Nature does.
So if Nature's temper is short-lived, then so should ours be.
To understand Nature, the Hunter must watch Nature.
Look for enlightenment and you will receive enlightenment.
Lose the trail and you will lose your Way.
At one with Nature, she will nurture and nourish you.
Look to the light and the light will guide you.
Take the wrong path and the path will engulf you.
If you cannot trust in Nature, you will not enjoy Her trust.

Nature has no concern in the consequence of Her actions. All of Her charges must learn to exist within Her moods. She may caress, nurture, warm, feed and water Her charges. Or she may soak, freeze, batter, swamp and starve Her charges. She has no enduring temper so nor should Her charges. Rage and cruelty have no place in the hunters psyche. He must act like Nature herself. He must view life and death without bias and deal death with efficiency, yet without guilt. If the Hunter follow Nature's Way and models his behaviour on Nature's examples he will follow a path which is wide and easily followed. If the Hunter leaves this path he risks being abandoned by Nature. The dark, winding, weed-strangled and miry trail of the cruel and the in-compassionate awaits him. This is a trail that leads to nowhere but sorrow and discontent. Follow the path trodden by the enlightened and the wise. Be guided along the track by Nature and she will hold your hand. She will lead your eye, open your ear and will enjoy the journey.

Twenty Four

Standing on tiptoes makes one unsteady.
The Hunter should keep his feet firmly planted.
Over-striding tires the legs. Keep a steady pace.
The wise Hunter walks in the shadows, shunning glare.
He avoids piety. It does not bring respect.
He never boasts as it brings no profit.
He never brags. Braggarts never endure.
To Nature's children, these things are superfluous.
They are waste and baggage, to be discarded.
They do not bring peace or contentment.
Therefore, the Hunter should avoid them.

The hunters most valuable attribute should be his silence and his stealth. To walk in the shadows, to strike and then to return to the shadows. Retreating into the background, removing yourself from attention to sit and watch is the hunters Way. Standing aloft, making yourself obvious, seeking attention? This is not for the Hunter. Strutting and bragging, displaying like a peacock? This is not for the Hunter. The wise Hunter stays level in head and steady in mind. Every movement is smooth and balanced. Every breath measured, every action calculated. Even inside life, outside the field and wood. The real Hunter will carry himself with dignity and modesty, distancing himself from renown or arrogance. These bring nothing, nor does Nature recognise them. Anything that Nature can ignore, the Hunter can ignore. They will bring nothing to his life. The Hunter needs nothing but affinity with Nature and the respect of his family and friends.

Twenty Five

A supreme mystery preceded the heavens and the earth.
Silent, vast, immeasurable. Unique and unchanging.
Always there, ever flowing, never faltering.
It birthed Nature, the mother of the billion things.
Some call the supreme mystery, the Way, the Way.
Because it is supreme, it is infinite.
That which is infinite, is perpetual.
Because the Way is great, the heavens are great.
Because the heavens are great, the earth is great.
Because the earth is great, mankind is great.
These are the four 'greatness's' of the universe.
The Hunter, part of Nature, is thus part of this.
The Hunter follows the laws of earth.
The earth follows the laws of the heavens.
The heavens follow the laws of the Way.
The Way dictates the laws of Nature.

The Hunter knows more than most the hierarchy and the design of the world in which he moves and Natures influence on the matters of the Earth and the atmosphere that sustains it. He would not deny the existence of a higher influence, beyond Earth, beyond the Moon, beyond the visible universe. Yet the Hunter, with his pragmatism and particularly his affinity with life and death, knows that we have no claim to that influence. To infer that we humans, simply because we are the highest intelligence in our own small sphere of existence, are at one with that supreme influence is pure arrogance. We are inconsequential in its grand design. Yet we are supremely important to the ecology of the planet on which we live. Therefore we must covenant to protect the Earth. We must defend its species and its environment for the benefit of all who follow us. The Hunter is not exempt from this responsibility. In fact it is often the Hunter who has the mandate for such care and responsibility. The Hunter, as an agent of Nature, often understands Nature and Her requirements far better than most. Only those who study and follow the laws and behaviours of Nature will get close to the Way. Life is a series of stepping stones across a turbulent stream. Some pass over, some fall, yet all have the chance to discover the Way. Find Nature and you have found the Way.

Twenty Six

Gravity anchors frivolity and lightness.
Tranquillity overcomes restlessness.
The Hunter, moving all day long,
Takes all that he needs, no more.
He will see wondrous things.
Yet he will remain composed and rational.
It would not become the Hunter, who wields such power.
To behave facetiously. The Hunter needs focus.
To lose ones gravity is to lose ones power.
To be restless and anxious is to lose control.

The Hunter applies a serious approach to his traverse of wood and field. He understands the consequence of his movement and presence, enjoying the experience while still ensuring that he tries to pass through the forest like the browsing fallow buck, silent and unseen. The Hunter will enjoy the privilege of witnessing much of Nature's wonder yet will keep his counsel on what he has seen. He knows where the hen pheasant sits tight on Her clutch. He watches the doe birth Her fawn and lay it in cover. He sees the hawk that watches the poults, yet exercises restraint. The mature Hunter never needs to take the 'percentage' shot. Every shot will be assessed, measured and executed with pure accuracy. To do any less is to trivialise the privilege which Nature has afforded. Two of the most effective tools of the Hunter are these ... composure and concentration.

Twenty Seven

The worthy stalker leaves no trail.
The skilled caller sounds like the creatures he mimics.
The proficient Hunter knows his ranges.
He needs no measure but his own trusty eye.
He sets the snare that cannot be slipped.
His hound is tied to him, not by a leash, but by his whisper.
The Hunter tends to his charges, abandons none.
He uses and preserves his catch. Nothing is wasted.
This is how he follows Nature. Enlightened and economic.
The good Hunter must be the poor Hunter's mentor.
For the poor Hunter simply wants to be a good Hunter.
What of those who disregard the offer of learning?
What of those who decline to teach those in need?
They will confuse Nature itself, for that is not Nature's Way.
Nature nurtures and she herself teaches. That is Her virtue.

The most admirable hunters are those who steal into and out of the landscape without being noticed. They leave no footprints, everything is left as it was found. They make no noise other than the sound of the wild itself. They can mimic the bird and the beast. The shot is judged for distance, for elevation and for windage in a fleeting moment. The trapper knows his art and nothing will escape. He will check his traps frequently to minimise distress. The Hunter puts all that falls to his attention to good use. The edible will be eaten and excess shared. The offal will be fed to his own beasts or to his wild counterparts. The hunters hound will be trained impeccably and respond to a whisper or a flick of the fingers. The admirable Hunter will teach all these things, willingly. They will, just as Nature does, share wisdom and knowledge. Those who refuse to teach will spoil Natures intention by allowing poor habit and bad practise. Those who refuse the offer of being taught do likewise. Nature will reject them and they will fail as hunters. The distribution of knowledge and wisdom is as crucial to Nature as the distribution of seed or spore. It ensures continuity and sustainability. It ensures that the circle of life is a closed loop. Every predator must also be prey. Even mankind. That is Natures Way.

Twenty Eight

Combine masculine detachment with feminine compassion.
Be like a river, flowing through your land.
Carve your path, like the rivers torrent. Unstoppable.
Yet open your mind to new experiences, like a young child.
Appreciate the light but hold to the shadow.
Set an example to all around you.
Being an example to all around you, be consistent.
You will gain infinite respect.
Accept praise and honour but remain humble.
Be like the apple tree in the orchard.
Let others pick the fruit that is your knowledge.
As they harvest your fruit, return to simplicity.
Start again. An un-carved block of timber.
Or the quill plucked from the goose.
When the timber is fashioned, it makes the gun stock or the bow.
The Hunter uses these to put food on the table.
Therefore, the timber feeds everyone.
When the quill is trimmed and dipped in ink.
It writes the book that teaches everyone.

The Hunter must be strong and determined. The taking of life, even for food or for necessity, should never sit easily in the mind. To stare down and feel sadness at the falling of a beautiful creature shows the mark of a true Hunter, a Hunter at one with Nature. Yet the Hunter will move through his obligations unrestrained by remorse or guilt. He will soak up new experience, fresh learning and the wisdom of others like a sponge. He will enjoy respect but never demand it. He will lead his life being an example of fair law and moderation. He will pass on his experience and his knowledge without harbouring secrets or claiming superiority. When he has shared this wisdom, he will return to the wild to learn more. Then he will share it again. The passing of knowledge and awareness will take many forms. Some hunters will be craftsman who can teach how to carve a bow or slingshot, how to make a snare or tunnel trap, how to make a bird-call. Other hunters will be specialists who can teach how to cast a fly-line, how to tickle a trout, how to run a long-net, how to set a decoy pattern. Everyone has it within them to pass on wisdom, no matter how trivial, so that successive generations sustain the self-sufficiency of hunting in all its forms. The old tribes and civilisations passed on such acumen by word of mouth, through the storyteller and the minstrel. Later it became the scribe and the illustrator. In modern times there are visual and social media. Whatever teaches can only benefit the new Hunter. Yet he must ensure it adheres to the oldest of hunting principles. Strength, determination, compassion, and fair law.

Twenty Nine

Some want to dominate and change Nature.
The Hunter knows this cannot be done.
Nature cannot be improved. She is perfect.
Those that attempt to, never succeed.
Nature will overcome Her challengers and ruin them.
Those who try to control Nature will be lost to Nature.
In Nature some things forge ahead, some are restrained.
Sometimes there is hard labour, sometimes respite.
Sometimes there is power, sometimes capitulation.
Sometimes there is growth, sometimes decay.
Sometimes the spirit is buoyant, at others drowning.
The Hunter must remain composed and avoid extremes.
The vigilant succeed. The complacent will fail.

The Hunter is often accused of illegitimate interference with Nature and Her charges yet nothing could be further from the truth. Man has been hunting since he first stood on two legs. Had he not, there would be no mankind today. The Hunter respects his place in Nature and interferes minimally, yet the folk who seek to vilify him meddle most with Nature and Her design. Nature doesn't hold Her wild creatures in cages so that folk can pay to see them. She doesn't stop the fox from stalking the coney. She doesn't stop the owl from hunting to vole. So why would she stop man from pursuing the fox? It is the blind ignorance and hypocrisy of folk who have never lived within Nature who castigate the Hunter and his place within Her strategy. The Hunter, like the mistress he serves, can understand life, death, work, play, growth and decay. The wise Hunter resists futile argument with those who believe death has no place in life's rich pageant. The passing of life sustains future life. The Hunter understands this therefore doesn't need to justify it. He applauds the fragility of existence and thus enjoys every moment of his own life.

Thirty

When teaching harmony within Nature.
Teach that cruelty is unacceptable and unwise.
Brutality rebounds on its user.
The soldier wages war, not the Hunter.
Any battlefield is devoid of crop or harvest.
It is the place of thorns and poppies, not bounty.
The Hunter takes what is needed, no more.
Hunt only for need, not excess.
Achieve results but don't glory in them.
Achieve results but don't flaunt them.
Achieve results yet remain modest.
Hunt only when the larder is empty or pests prevail.
Harvest or control but don't annihilate.
Surplus ... too often ... results in famine.
Nature abhors imbalance. Don't promote imbalance.
For that which defies Nature cannot endure

The Hunter should always act with a sense of purpose woven around a sense of compassion ... and should teach such sensitivity too. He should lead by example and school his understudies to avoid cruelty or brutality. To respect and honour the lives they seek to take. The work of the Hunter is not war. His quarry is not an enemy in the true sense of the word, for his quarry is incapable of bearing malice towards him. Even the alpha predator, capable of harming the Hunter, will never do so through malevolence. It will only do so in self-defence or fear. The good Hunter, stalking for food, takes only what is needed or can be shared. He shouldn't brag or glorify in his achievements but instead behave discreetly and with respect to those who fail to understand his ways. Don't flaunt the catch or the harvest in front of those who could take offence. The efficient Hunter also acts with frugality in the garnering of food. He will rotate his land as a farmer rotates his crops. He will ensure that he leaves behind enough of the crop to assure sustainability and further hunting. Obliteration serves no useful purpose unless life is threatened by disease or pollution. The edible are only edible if they can be hunted. Eradication of quarry is like the burning of a forest or the blocking of the water-well. Hunger and thirst will triumph.

Thirty One

The bow and the rifle are menacing tools.
Many of the billion things shrink from them.
Yet the Hunter and the soldier are privileged use them.
The Hunter, to supply food and to protect crops.
The soldier, to guard his nation and monarch.
Battalions are instruments of defence and necessity.
Such arms are only used when there is disharmony.
The wise prefer peace and neutrality.
Victory should be accepted without glory.
Glorification displays a delight in death.
Those who delight in death are not at one with Nature.
When the world is at peace, the Hunter's rifle is a simple tool.
When the world is at war, the soldiers' rifle is a harsh weapon.
The Hunter sits on the left, the soldier on the right.
Yet both have the same attitude to their role.
Both kill with reluctance and only through necessity.
Neither glorify in the deed. Both treat it sombrely.

The Hunter is often described as carrying a weapon yet nothing is further from the truth. A weapon is an instrument or device used in combat, fighting or war. The Hunter is not at war. In the hands of the Hunter a rifle or bow ... or any other device ... is a tool. A tool designed to assist him accomplish his task with efficiency, mercy and compassion. In the hands of the soldier a rifle or bow ... or any other device ... is a weapon. It is designed to assist in the defence of king and country, which may involve the taking of human life. Both Hunter and soldier know how to kill yet neither will relish the prospect. The skill, the discipline and the control of the Hunter and the soldier are identical. The taking of one life for the preservation of many others is mutual to both. The need for common sense, caution and moral responsibility sits equally with both. Many would say it is the soldier whose conscience will be tested more by the requirement to kill. But is this true? The wise always work towards peace and harmony therefore the soldier may serve a lifetime without have to make the decision to kill. The Hunter will be faced with the decision thousands of times. Therefore the Hunter must never lose sight of the moral significance of his task. The Hunter whose ten hundredth kill tests his conscience as much as his first kill? That is a true Hunter, at one with Nature. The Hunter whose ten hundredth kill feels cold and impassive? He is not a Hunter. He is an assassin.

Thirty Two

The Way is indefinable, it is simplicity.
Nothing can grasp it. Even Nature cannot influence it.
If the wise could conquer it?
The billion things would be at their command.
The universe and Nature would combine.
Everything would unite in harmony.
Mankind would need not interfere, all would just 'be'.
The billion things have all been named.
Names are everywhere, for everything.
When the named things become extinct?
When Nature is in reverse, we need to understand why?
Mankind needs to heed its cause of disharmony.
The Way needs to flow forward, like a stream to the sea.
If the Way flows backwards, like the sea into the river.
The billion things wither and die.
Mankind is one of the billion things.

Life's deepest mystery, the answer to the query that supersedes all questions, is mind-bending. Men have gone mad trying fathom the answer. What came before the planets and the suns and the black void of space? What birthed the universe? The question is a futile one for such a low form in the Ways intentions as mankind. If we were important enough, then we would know, would we not? Lives have been wasted, wars have been enacted and societies have been built ... and destroyed ... by those claiming that their answer to the question is the right one and the only one. Such is the arrogance of mankind. We have every right to try to understand Nature, for she nurtures us. What birthed Her should be irrelevant to us. Until we learn how to respect Nature, how dare we seek to understand any higher order? We, mankind, explore Nature and we set about labelling every living organism while, at the same time, we destroy it's environment and then record it's extinction with dismay. Rather than define deity and pretentiously argue righteousness and piety, surely mankind would be better served to address the immediate, the present, within Nature? Does the kingfisher ask where the river leads? It matters not. Does the hare ask what birthed the crop upon which it feeds? Its life doesn't depend on the answer. It depends on the crop being there, now.

Thirty Three

Understanding bird, beast, flower and insect is wisdom.
Understanding yourself is enlightenment.
Mastering bird and beast requires discipline.
Conquering your own self-control is true power.
Knowing when you have harvested enough.
That is truly knowing the value of your bounty.
Self-motivation and perseverance display will-power.
The Hunter should be like the mighty tree.
He should set deep roots and reside where he grows.
Like the tree, even in death, he will endure.
Visible to all and a Way-mark to all who come after.

The Hunter will never be proficient unless he can identify species at a glance. More than that, they need to understand their quarry intimately. The Hunter needs to know where his quarry feeds, what it feeds upon, what it preys on, what preys on his quarry? Where does it nest, where does it breed and birth? When does it feed, or breed? In knowing his quarry, the Hunter will also know all other living things. His attention will be drawn to the worm and the tick as much as to the deer and the wolf. To be part of Nature he needs to understand the eco-system in which he hunts on Her behalf. Knowing everything about what he may be called upon to cull isn't sufficient. He needs to know cause and effect, opportunity and consequence. Therefore the Hunter should be parochial. He should set roots and walk the same ground constantly. Most of all, the Hunter needs to understand his own ability, temperament and self-control.

Thirty Four

Nature's energy flows through everything, in all directions.
She penetrates every fissure, every pore, like rushing water.
The billion things depend on Her tirelessness.
She nurtures everything but demands no nurture herself.
Nature is the life force of the billion things.
Yet she holds no dominion.
Making no demands, she needs no sustenance.
She is formless. She needs no space to exist.
The billion things that come from Her, return to Her.
That is Nature's potency. The virtuous circle.
That is why Nature is wondrous.
Because Nature claims no supremacy, she is truly supreme.

The evidence of the existence of a higher order which orchestrates life is all around the Hunter. He can't smell Her or hear Her or see Her or taste Her ... but he witnesses both the miracles and the calamity she can command. We call Her Nature and as well as life or death, she controls the elements of air, earth, fire and water to either sustain or subdue Her charges. She is everywhere. Like the dandelion seed that disperses on the breeze, she floats in the air and settles in every void. Like the cascade of the waterfall she drives Her strength behind the flow of creation. Nature demands nothing in return. Like the Way, which birthed Her, she seeks no sanctity. Nature needs no sacrifice and demands no reverence. She has no use for temples or spires or churches. Nature expects life to be lived to its full and death to be accepted with honour. All living things issued by Her, will return to Her. No living thing escapes this cycle. Nature asks for no space yet gifts space for all things to exist through this action.

Thirty Five

The Hunter, to be part of Nature, must blend with his environment.
All Nature's creatures will pass him by, unconcerned.
The Hunter may copy the creatures call.
The Hunter might bait with food.
If he contradicts Nature, his deceptions will fail.
Look at Nature. Can you see Her?
Listen to Nature. Can you hear Her?
Replicate Nature. Use Nature. Her wisdom is immeasurable.

Many hunters confuse camouflage with a dress code. In the monochrome world of most wild creatures the colours we wear are insignificant so long as they blend into the local surroundings. Dark against dark and light against light. It is the skill of slipping into deep shadow when necessary, of moving through the forest or along the hedgerows shade unmarked. The ambitious Hunter will listen and learn how to mimic, not just his quarry but also it's prey. He will know how to lay bait in a manner that convinces it's intended benefactor. Being part of Nature is rarely about looking like Nature. Being part of Nature is about understanding what Natures charges looks like and what they sound like.

Thirty Six

To thin something, one must first fatten it.
Let the rabbit warren fill, then just take what you need.
To benefit from weakening something, it must first be strong.
Like the mighty tree felled for timber.
To harvest a crop, you must first feed and nurture it.
To gain from something, one must first give to it.
That is Nature's golden rule. She cannot take what she hasn't given.
For the Hunter, subtlety and respect for quarry must endure .
The pike, a high predator, feeds in deep water for good reason.
The Hunter puts food on the table without glorying how it got there.

The Hunter cannot simply extract from Nature with also putting something back in. The Hunter, like the farmer, must also nourish and cultivate. He will overlook the rabbit kits and cull the adults. He will ensure that there is a balance of male and female to sustain the warren. He will close in swiftly on disease and protect the warren from other high predators. He will ensure the balance between buck and doe in the roe herd is measured and he will respect the seasons. That relationship with quarry must hold high importance on the hunters agenda, for Nature is watching him. The good Hunter doesn't over-cull, nor does he openly exhibit his craft. This is common to most high predators. The leopard hauls Her catch into a tree to feed. The Hunter dresses out his shot quarry with discretion and respect. No-one should ever need know he was abroad.

Thirty Seven

Nature's unceasing influence is invisible.
Yet everything is happening, nothing is forgotten.
If the Hunter waits patiently, Nature will unfold.
The billion things will thrive under Nature's guidance.
Nature will orchestrate and harmonise.
Balance follows and the world is at peace.

Nature never hurries in Her tasks yet everything is accomplished, as designed, always. That is part of Nature's eternal beauty. Her consistency. The Hunter will see nothing, yet see everything. He won't see some ethereal wraith moving among the naked boughs of Winters trees but he will awake to see the Spring snowdrops carpeting the woodland floor. He will hear the robin serenading his hen. He will watch Summers butterflies emerge from the chrysalis and he will watch Nature's pastels paint the Autumn wood.

Thirty Eight

The proficient Hunter doesn't dwell on his ability.
Yet the incompetent Hunter overestimates his aptitude.
The expert Hunter deploys little energy, all comes naturally.
He achieves success with economy and simplicity.
The inept Hunter is a busy fool, achieving little.
The benevolent Hunter acts with thought and compassion.
In doing so, none of his charges suffer unduly.
The cruel Hunter acts on a poor agenda.
Suffering and brutality will follow.
When the concept of Natural law is lost.
The good and compassionate are displaced.
Cruelty and suffering are viewed as the norm.
Righteousness and ritual substitute for Natural law.
Those who misunderstand Nature take control.
Those who purport to know Nature, fail it.
They see only the value of life, not the purity of death.
Foolishness and false teaching prevail.
The good Hunter, Nature's true follower.
Sees the pragmatic, not the romantic.
He anticipates the fruit, that follows the flower, that follows the seed.
He accepts only true Nature, not its false representation.

As with all ways of life, experience brings confidence to the Hunter and his craft becomes second-Nature. He takes time to study and to train, improving his skills. The hunters world is full of imitators who try to bypass the long apprenticeship which is so vitally required to become a *sensei*. Many will kill to achieve a tally rather than for just purpose. The unpractised are the inaccurate. They attempt to hunt yet fail to achieve a standard which minimises suffering and thus they act cruelly. Many folk think their actions are the norm and so all hunters are tarred with the same brush. The people rally behind folk with a misplaced sense of morality. Folk who cannot understand that a pure life demands a pure death. Folk who don't even understand death. Not all death is 'cruel'. Cruelty is indifference to suffering and the good Hunter is never indifferent. Laws are enacted which oppose the laws of Nature, by agents who neither know Nature nor act on Her behalf. The scavenger, the thief and the predator become the protected while the vulnerable enjoy no defence. The general populace, expecting that such laws are lain down the wise, believe this false propaganda. No law that pitches man against man is representative of Nature's Way. The Hunter will hold to the truth and continue his art, yet perhaps with more discretion. He will act like the fox or the raptor. He will retire from the vicinity of those who seek to attack him. To argue or debate with the misinformed and the prejudiced is futile. Far better for the Hunter to stay his tongue and retreat into his work. Confrontation achieves nothing. Inaction will triumph over action. The Hunter should ignore false laws and misguided ethics. He must concentrate on Nature and Her laws, for they always prevail over man-kinds often senseless statutes.

Thirty Nine

So what arose within the Way, so long ago?
The heavens arose, complete and clear.
The earth arose, whole and firm.
Nature arose, limitless and potent.
The wilderness arose, vast and abundant.
The billion things were created, Nature's purpose.
Mankind arose within this, thus nations arose.
None of these would exist without the Way.
The heavens, without its force, would collapse.
The earth, without its support, would implode.
Nature, without the Ways mandate, would vanish.
The wilderness, without Nature's spirit, would perish.
The billion things would wither and die.
Mankind is one of the billion things.
Mankind has a duty of care over the billion things.
Without them, Nature has no purpose.
Without Nature, the earth and the heavens have no purpose.
Without these, the Way would dismiss us.
Mankind needs to accept this humility in Nature.

Mankind has tried since its inception to find an explanation for the imperceptibility of time and the immeasurability of the universe. The ancient sages reasoned nearly three millennia ago that these matters were beyond the comprehension of man. So why waste time worrying about these historic conundrums? Surely it is far more sensible to simply accept the simple truths rather than seek to concoct theories and manufacture doctrines to support and sustain them? Accept that there is an intelligence, a power , a Way which holds all of the universe we know in its custody. It sustains the earth, the planets, the stars and all the space between them. It delegates the control of life to the force we call Nature. If the Way retreated, Nature and the universe would collapse. If Nature withdrew, all life would perish. The Hunter understands this yet many of his kindred fail to see that the force of Nature is far more important to serve than the Way itself. To stand in awe of the Way is understandable and laudable. To pay homage to the Way, to build shrines, to claim unity with the Way, to expect perpetual existence within the Way? Surely this is arrogance? Mankind, like the Hunter, should live humbly within Nature and tend to the earthly, not the ethereal. If all things perish without Natures presence then it is our task to help protect Nature and Her charges. Without those charges, Nature has no purpose. If Nature has no purpose and withdraws back into the Way then the universe will follow Her. The earth, the stars and the space will have no use. We will be no more. Life will cease to be important to the Way.

Forty

Nature's Way displays a virtuous circle.
The growth and the withering.
The spring bud, autumns falling leaf.
The strong overcoming the weak.
The mayfly that hatches, mates and dies.
The salmon returning upriver to spawn before death.
The billion things grow, exist, procreate, expire.
Their death is inconsequential.
They have already created new life, new being.
They are therefore virtuous, like Nature, like the Way.

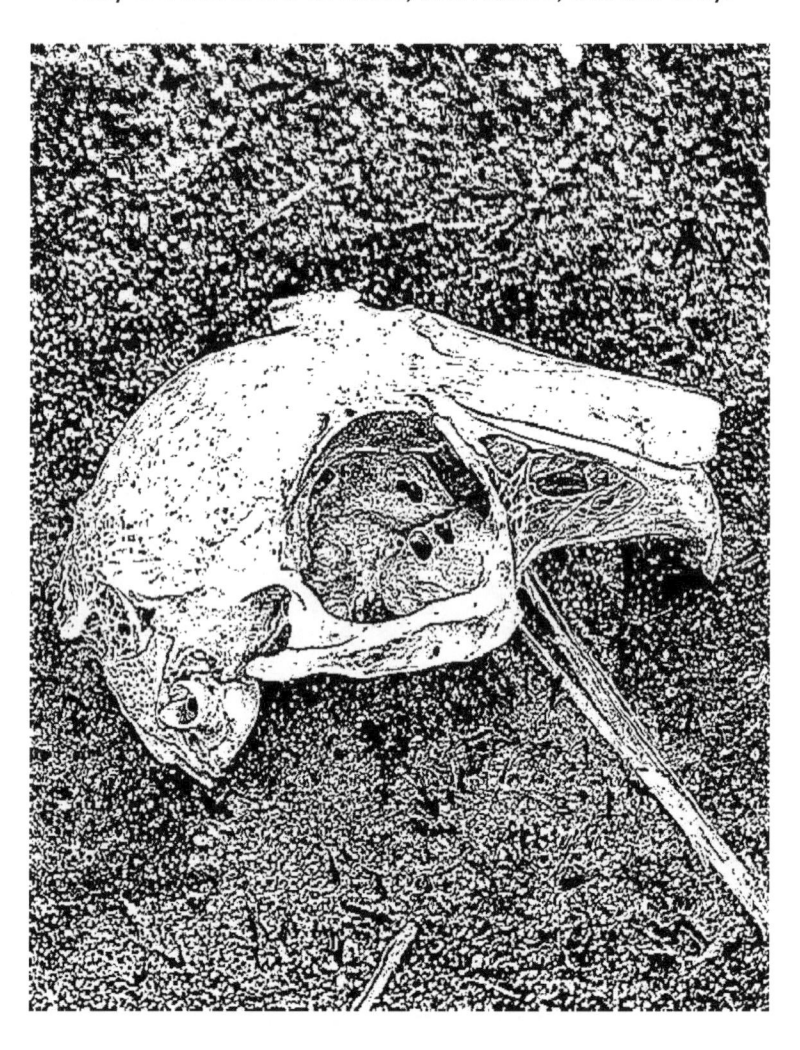

The Hunter appreciates the circle of life more than most, for he is often instrumental in it. Longevity or brevity of life is of no consequence to Nature so nor should it be to the Hunter. It is the living of the life that is important, not how it ends. Many folk forget that the Hunter saves more lives than he takes. Many folk forget that the Hunter feeds many, therefore sustains life. This is all part of his significance within Nature. The Hunter himself will be subject to the same uncertainty as to the duration of his life as all Natures other creatures. He has no mandate or exemption to preclude him from Natures virtuous circle, yet the Hunter has something special indeed. The Hunter has the benefit of watching all of Natures phenomena. The Hunter loves life, for he sustains life. He doesn't fear death, for he is death. His own will come when Nature decrees it.

Forty One

The wise Hunter listens closely to Nature.
The mediocre Hunter listens at will.
The poor Hunter dismisses Nature and mocks Her.
Nature does not discriminate. She is above that.
She exists for the wise, the mediocre and the poor.
The clearest path may seem the dullest.
Moving forwards may feel like going backwards.
The easy trail may prove wearisome.
The virtuous Way may feel unexciting.
Therefore, high morals feel worthless.
The profit from morality seems low.
So the point of being virtuous feels frail.
It seems the right Way brings no reward?
Remember though, a perfect square has no corners.
The best skills are learned through experience.
The sweetest song is the one hardest to hear.
The most beautiful form has no definition.
The Way is unseen, invisible.
The Way, alone, nourishes Nature.
And Nature brings everything to fulfilment.

Nature is impartial, oblivious to ability or intelligence or health. She has no bias, no discrimination. Large, small, fit, unfit, male, female, young, old. None of these are important to Nature. To move forward under Natures guidance may not entail pure wonder or enlightenment. Sometimes Nature takes you forward on a plain and simple trail. Yet if you trust Her she will take you where you want to be. Often the Hunter will be looked upon with disdain. A plain man living a simple life. People will say 'What did you do this week?' and he will reply 'I walked the field and the wood'. They will turn away to discuss their television programs, their shopping trip, their restaurant meal or their dinner party. The Hunter will smile quietly to himself. What did he do in the field and in the wood? He watched and wondered and learned. He listened to the yellow buntings song and heard the bark of the roebuck in deep cover. The Hunter heard the early cuckoo and saw the first swallow. He looked upon the blackcaps chicks in their nest and scoured the nearby scene for sign of magpie and jay, burglars both, who would relish the taste of such sweet and tender flesh. He sat to watch the trout hold beneath the chalk-streams gentle flow, leaping to snatch the mayfly hatchling. He witnessed the vixens short, low-bellied stalk toward the warren and saw Her miss the sprightly rabbit kit. The Hunter passed the grass snake coiled, sunbathing, on the tussock. He watched the fierce bout as two cock pheasants fought for realm and harem. The Hunter watched, smelt and heard the reality and purity of Nature as the Way intended. Not for him the shallow, materialistic and two-dimensional world of those who scorn his ways.

Forty Two

The Way created the heavens and the earth.
The Way created Nature, which birthed the billion things.
The billion things carry yin and hold yang.
These two combine to create harmony and longevity.
Ebb and flow, dark and light, birth and death, give and take.
People dislike being opposed, misunderstood or detested.
Yet the Hunter must often walk that path.
He gains by casting off misplaced conscience and ignorance.
He loses the burden of false morality and un-Natural law.
The Hunter accepts the teaching of the ancients.
Live within Nature and you will die within Nature.
Live compassionately and your passing will be compassionate.
Live cruelly and you will die cruelly. That is Nature's Way.

The concept of yin (the female) and yang (the male) abounds in ancient culture. The balance of opposites. Male and female. Light and dark. Good and evil. Ebb and flow. Birth and death. High and low. This is Natures Way. Balance within the Way is vital to its harmony and the Hunter must accept this. Therefore the Hunter and his ways will be opposed. Just as the Hunter will oppose ways contrary to his own belief and lifestyle. Such opposing views are healthy and are the advocacy put in place by Nature to ensure that for every view there is a counter-view. The Hunter must accept this. Yet he will gain comfort in his knowledge of bird and beast, of life and death, of predator and prey. Most of all he will carry no malice towards those who hold opposing views, indeed different interpretations, of Natures intentions. The Hunter will let Nature herself hold the gavel. Nature alone can ensure that Her objectives are met. The Hunter will hold to Her Way and resist conflict. If he lives honestly within Nature, she will oblige him with an honourable death. If he lives cruelly, then Nature will abandon him.

Forty Three

The softest things in the universe overcome the hardest.
Heat and cold can break rock and ice, yet they have no form.
Things without substance can fill the vacuous space.
Water flows into the fissure, mist fills the ravine.
Thus the Hunter should recognise the value of inaction.
Sometimes the passive option is the most powerful option.
Often, it is what the Hunter does lightly that proves most potent.
He makes no move. He makes no sound. He takes no shot.
He is like the watching falcon and the falcon never starves.
He returns home with an empty bag, yet more wisdom.
Can you see the value of such inaction?
Few but the wise understand this.

Nature shows us in many ways how intangibility can wield awesome power over the tangible. The gentle trickle of water that over millennia can cut a gorge through solid rock, yet no man can grasp it. The gale that fells the forest timber can be heard but not held between the fingers. Nature demonstrates, therefore, that power has nothing to do with substance. The fog that creeps between the tree boles and the mist that hangs in the autumn vale cannot be grasped. Yet they fill our vision like the timber and the ravine. The Hunter must learn from these examples. To act gently but relentlessly can often carve the path we wish to follow. Sagacity and wisdom are won by seizing the mist. Watch the mist, try to understand its formlessness, accept that you cannot catch it. It will clear. When it does, you will appreciate what was hidden behind it. Knowledge of Nature is like that. Only by studying Her will you understand how all Her charges can function. Understanding will burn through just as the sun burned through the mist.

Forty Four

Status or sanity. Which is the most important?
The peacock's suit serves little purpose but to pose.
The cock pheasant's finery looks drab as he hangs in the larder.
Health or wealth. Which is the most precious?
Rich and chained … or poor and free?
Gain or loss. Which brings the most pain?
The more you possess, the more you stand to lose.
Only the greedy can suffer heavy loss.
Accept what you have and you cannot be disappointed.
Know when your pot is full and enjoy the feast.
Respect your home for the security it gives you.
When you know you have enough, the desire for more won't press you.
You will remain content and secure.

The drive for prestige and admiration is seldom a trait which is associated with the Hunter. Simplicity and modesty will be his fashion. The dowdy jackdaw is less pursued than the gaudy jay or flamboyant magpie. The Hunter enjoys all the riches that Nature freely offers and scorns the need for homely treasures. His assets are those needed for the accomplishment of his work. He will place more importance in the strength to walk the hill and forest ride than the value of accumulated wealth. Those who possess little are free to walk with abandon and to seek adventure. Those with riches dare not leave them unattended or guarded for they are possessive. Own little and none can take from you. Own much and you can lose hugely. The Hunter will look about him and take vast pleasure from sight, sound, scent and Natural bounty. His cottage is his castle, though he need not lock the gates. Satisfaction comes through useful existence, not from the relentless climb to be prominent and esteemed. Security comes through anonymity not through celebrity. Wealth is relative to need, as the Hunter well knows.

Forty Five

The Hunter may feel that great success feels hollow.
The sight of fallen quarry may test the conscience.
This is a triumph. Feeling fulfilled, yet feeling empty.
That is a state that the Hunter should always endure.
These are emotions that only mankind can feel.
The right Way can feel like the wrong Way.
The artisan skill can feel brutal and archaic.
The classical teaching can seem awkward.
The cold Hunter will keep mobile, induce heat.
The warm Hunter will move little, encourage coolness.
When the forest is in turmoil, the Hunter will retreat silently.
Inactivity, tranquillity, silence .. these restore order to disorder.
Nature allows us conscience, decision, action, inaction.
These are a blessing from Nature.

There is no glory in the taking of a wild creatures life, there is only accomplishment. Nature herself is responsible for the taking of a billion lives every day. She births the gene that grows the virus or the cancer. She raises or lowers the temperature. She shakes the earth that moves the tsunami. She fans the wind that spreads the forest fire. Most importantly, she signs the mandate that allows the predator to hunt. Mankind is an alpha predator, indicted to hunt on his and Natures behalf. Those that oppose this obvious acquiescence by Nature insult Her authority. The true Hunter walks the field and wood with high conscience yet low emotion. The fox doesn't cry over the chickens demise. The owl doesn't weep as it clasps the wood-mouse. The heron doesn't sing dirges for the bream. The Hunter may look down on his quarry with satisfaction at the crisp and merciful execution but with regret at the loss of such wondrous life. With joy at the filling of the cook-pot but with melancholy at how it is filled. This is what puts mankind above all other predators under Natures responsibility. The choice been action and inaction on moral grounds. We are the only creature blessed with conscience.

Forty Six

When Nature is in balance and the Way is stable.
Men farm and machines are used to plough and to harvest.
When mankind disrupts Nature, it disrupts the Way.
Then men fight and machines become weapons of war.
Poppies adorn the cold stone memorials.
Nothing disturbs Nature more than craving and malcontent.
Nothing promotes misdeed more than coveting what others own.
The contented are those who know they already have enough.

Nature is delegated the responsibility for balance within the Way and she moves swiftly to redress dis-harmony. Nature does not reward conflict. She abandons it and so the battlefield becomes a place of desolation. Gravestones and wooden crosses stand in the place of flower and tree. Where man lives and toils in tune with Nature, she honours him with growth and harvest. He enjoys abundance and security. Greed, jealousy, piety and infamy are the triggers to war and invasion. Nature cares not what name the Way is given nor how mankind chooses to honour it. Conflict and argument in the name of the Way is contrary to the Way, therefore Nature will subtly oppose the contestants.

Forty Seven

Stepping outdoors does not guarantee understanding Nature.
Nor can one expect to see Her miracles simply by looking.
The further you delve into Her mystery.
The less likely you are to comprehend Her.
The wise Hunter knows, without asking.
He sees clearly, without looking.
He achieves his purpose in Nature without trying.

Too many people walk through Nature without even understanding that she is there. Nature is not the tree or the grass or the flower or the insect. Nature is not the earth or the sky or the mountain or the river. Folk call all these things Nature yet the Hunter knows this to be false. Nature is the driving force behind all life and, indeed, death. Look at the tree and all you will see is leaf and wood. Look at the floor and see the tiny two-leafed sprig, then look up at the huge bole alongside. How did the feeble sprig become the mighty oak tree? The answer is what no-one can see or touch. Nature.

Forty Eight

The gathering of wisdom means gaining something every day.
Understanding the Way means giving something back every day.
Sow, nourish, harvest, share, enrich, sow again.
Pair, breed, nurture, teach, release, pair again.
Nature's virtuous circle, over and over, eternally.
The more you relinquish, the less you need or desire.
The less you need or desire, the richer you become.
Nature embraces those who don't impede Her purpose.
Impede Her purpose and she will sweep you aside.

Every day that the Hunter spends in field and wood enriches his knowledge and his understanding of Nature and Her methods. He will see the courtship rituals, look upon the clutch of eggs and watch the fledglings learning to fly. The Hunter will note the caching of the acorn, the sprout of the twig and growth of the sapling. He will protect and nurture, encourage and teach. The Hunter needs little more than to witness these simple wonders and to play his part in them. He becomes rich in experience and wise in the intention of Nature. The Hunter will never fear Nature. He knows that she will shield him and also that if she chooses not to, then she has just purpose. The Hunter is often, therefore, as vulnerable as the chick he seeks to protect. Nature, alone, decides his fate.

Forty Nine

The wise Hunter is broad minded.
Yet is conscious of the feelings of others.
He is benevolent to those who show benevolence.
Yet also benevolent to those who do not.
For benevolence is the virtue, not its receipt.
He is faithful to those who show faith.
Yet also faithful to those who do not.
For faith is the virtue, not its reciprocation.
The wise exist in Nature, humbly.
Their minds become as unsullied as Nature.
Other people look to the wise for guidance.
Thus the wise should share their wisdom.

The Hunter will see much in the wild that would cause concern to many folk. He will, himself, act in a manner not approved by those who fail to understand his role. Thus he will seek to act with discretion. He may see cruelty and death enacted by others. His place is not to judge but to teach the rightful Way. To with-hold teaching and correction is against Natures laws. He will show the inaccurate shooter the Way to despatch cleanly. The Hunter shows kindness to the weak and the passive, yet also to the strong and resistant. It is the kindness that matters, not its benefactor. He will free the injured, snarling fox from the barbed wire. He will end the misery of the sickly coney. The Hunter will watch all around him with the vigilance of the little owl. Like the owl, his wisdom lies in seeing all yet judging nothing and no-one. In watching, he learns. In learning, he becomes wise. In wisdom, he understand. In understanding, he can therefore teach. To teach, to pass on the wisdom to others is one of the hunters greatest attributes.

Fifty

It is said that three in ten folk live for life.
And that three in ten folk dwell on death.
Another three in ten drift aimlessly from birth to death.
Why do they behave like this?
Because they live shallow and meaningless lives.
So what of the tenth of the ten people?
These draw huge richness from life.
They do not fear the wild because they are the wild.
Nature cannot harm them because they are part of Nature.
Nothing can pain them as they have no fear of pain.
Like the wild animal, only the present moment is important.
Death holds no terror, thus they lead a fulfilled life.

The Hunters Way draws on the one in ten. The three in ten that live for life only, live to excess. Their life will be self-serving and shallow. An accumulation of material wealth and extravagance. The three that dwell on death do so because they lack the confidence or foresight to enjoy the present. The glass will be half-full. The next day will always be better, yet never comes. Their god will deliver their bliss, after life. The three that drift aimlessly do so because they have no purpose, no ambition, no understanding of the value of both life and death. The Hunter spurns all such nonsense. He draws deep breath and marches into the wild to see and learn and live and understand. He stretches his muscle and heart and lungs and mind. The Hunter accepts that his place within Nature is limited to his life. So living, not worrying about death, is imperative to his fulfilment. In the wild, he is wild. In Nature, he is Nature. In life, he is the epitome of living. In death, he is nothing. He knows this, so enjoys every breath and every moment,

Fifty One

The billion things arise from the Way.
Nature nourishes the billion things.
They are tangible, visible, formed from matter.
Their environment shapes and influences them.
The billion things, respecting the Way, follow Nature's ways.
Respect for the Way and following Nature's ways are not demanded.
Yet the Way and Nature treat all equitably.
Thus the billion things are produced by the Way, birthed by Nature.
They grow, learn, evolve, mature, are protected.
Nature births without possessing, acts without asking repayment.
She claims no dominion over Her creations.
This is Nature's principal virtue.

Evolution is one of the greatest wonders that the Way has bestowed on all living things under Natures guidance. The ability of a species to adapt to environment, climate, landscape, food source or threat. Nature assists but does not prescribe. She allows without being asked. She protects without smothering. Nature demands no payment and oversees without reigning. The evolutionary process she supervises shows no bias. It is equitable and is proved so by the emergence of some species and the extinction of others. So if the Way and Nature has blessed Her charges with survival through evolution, how can anyone dare challenge that Nature gifted mankind the ability to become the ultimate predator? For she also gifted him conscience with which to act with responsibility and honesty. Had she not bestowed that gift our ancestors would never have stood on two legs. Mankind would never have mastered fire, tools and the basic weapons homo sapiens designed and developed to survive as a species.

Fifty Two

Nature herself began with the Way.
We regard Nature as the mother of the billion things.
Only when you find the mother.
Can you understand the daughters and sons.
Knowing the billion things, remaining in touch with Nature.
This what allays fear of death and frees the spirit of life.
Speak seldom, pass without noise, remain watchful.
And you will see everything in Nature without effort.
Pass rowdily, meddle, fuss, fidget and fret.
And you will never indulge in Nature's feast.
Seeing that which most ignore? That is real insight.
Restraining from force, controlling emotion? That is strength.
Use this enlightenment to gain clarity of purpose.
Achieve this self-control and you emulate Nature's constancy.

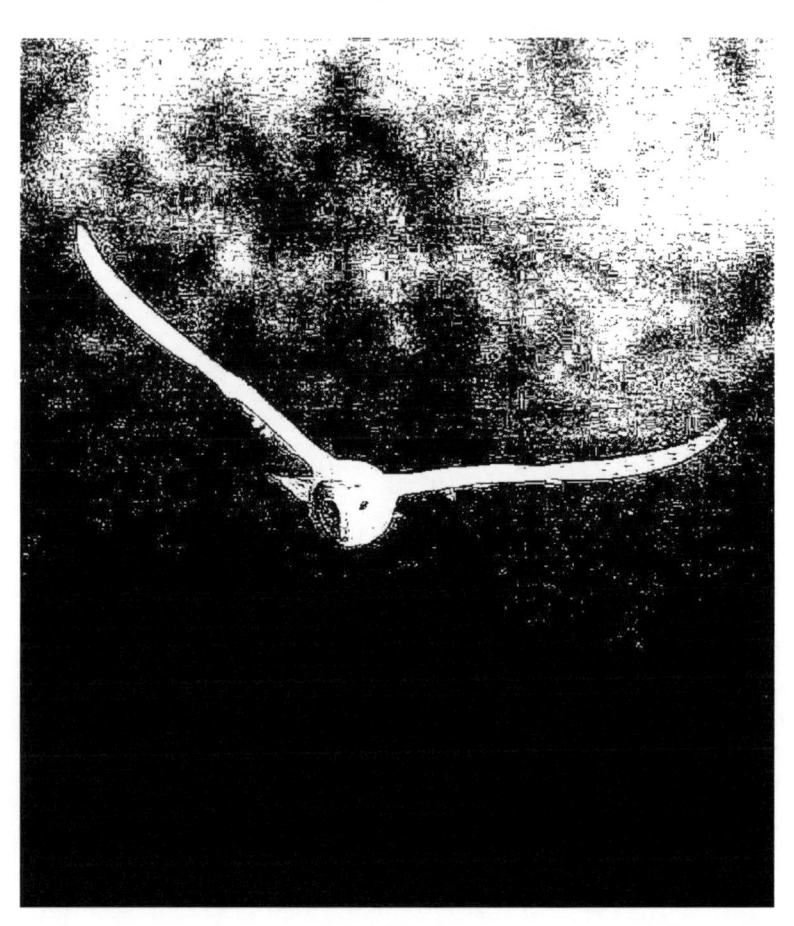

The Hunter enjoys a close understanding of Nature and the living things she supports. Part of the hunters skill is his ability to read a creatures intent and therefore that of his quarry. Most wild creatures are guided in their daily lives by Nature. They fly, walk, feed and breed according to Her timetable. The rise and fall of the sun, the phase of the moon, the cycle of the seasons, the famine and the drought. The Hunter, knowing Nature, knows how his quarry and its prey will act at these times. He will know the creatures habit, habitat, food and its lair or nest. Thus the Hunter will walk the wood in silence and watch. He will keep to the shadows seeing activity and behaviour that few enjoy. What the Hunter will see will serve to accentuate his role and purpose within this grand design. He will seek to attain the silence of the quartering owl, the vision of the heron, the hearing of the roebuck, the accuracy of the stooping falcon, the invisibility of the adder and the cunning of the fox. Yet the Hunter, even if achieving all such qualities, will have one advantage gifted him by Nature. He will have emotion. The use of restraint and the checking of conscience make the Hunter unique within Nature.

Fifty Three

The sensible will follow Nature's Way.
Their only fear should be straying from it.
Keeping to Nature's road is so simple.
Yet many stray from the path.
If our governance is greedy and materialistic.
The fields will be full of scrub and weed.
The cattle sheds and grain barns will be empty.
The sails on the windmill will stand idle.
Nobility will flaunt their achievement and finery.
Wealth will be used to bully and corrupt.
Spirituality will give Way to debauchery and excess.
This is despotism. It is contrary to Nature's example.

Mankind must understand that if Nature has bestowed evolutionary dominance to mankind then we would do well to respect Her judgement. Too many folk abandon Nature for the accumulation of fiscal wealth, material possession and property. The countryside needs modest infrastructure. The town, the city and the factory needs more. The politician, the economist and the industrialist must remember that when respect for natural resource declines, Nature herself will seek to restore balance. Man must never transfer his need to greed or his existence to affluence, at Natures cost. He will eventually pay the price for such folly, as history has constantly demonstrated. How many nations rise and fall watched by the forest and the mountain? How many rulers sit beneath the same mighty oak tree during its life? How many are buried side by side beneath the old yew tree in the graveyard? Even the carrion crow, unscathed by the Hunter, will outlive a politicians term in office. Trust in Nature. She endures.

Fifty Four

Deep, broad roots will anchor the tree against the storm.
A firm, tight grasp will thwart acquiescence.
These need to be taught down the generations.
Cultivate Nature within yourself and it will be genuine.
Plant it within the family and it will flourish.
Sow it within the community and it will prevail.
Grow it within the nation and Nature will be abundant.
See everybody as you see yourself.
See your family as like other families.
See your community as typical.
Accept other nations as you do your own nation.
All are part of Nature. All are part of the Way.
How does the Hunter know that Nature responds like this ?
The answer is simple. Because he watches Nature!

The Hunter understands the importance of stoicism. The most resilient survivors in Nature are those who either set down roots or those who build a community. Strong, embedded roots in the tree make it resistant to gale and torrent. Strong, entrenched roots in mankind provide law, values and wise governance. The concept of community and family within Nature is important. The Hunter can see why this is so. The mature protect the young. The strong feed the weak. The wise teach the uneducated. Nature is full of examples that demonstrate the relationship between fortitude and longevity. Sit and watch the rookery, the perfect illustration of this concept. The rooks build their nests high in solid trees with deep roots. The rookery is a vibrant, industrious hub from which the birds hunt for food for miles around and share knowledge of feeding sources with their neighbours. The birds send out raiding parties yet leave sentries behind to guard the chicks. The long established rookery is a sign that all is well with Nature in the locality. If the rookery is abandoned, it is because Nature is in disharmony. The food sources have been withdrawn. The agriculture has been forsaken.

Fifty Five

The confident Hunter walks through Nature like an innocent.
He doesn't fear the insect's sting or the viper's strike.
He doesn't fear the wild beast, for it is Nature's beast.
The soaring falcon holds no terror.
Though the flesh is weak and the bones are brittle.
His trust in Nature is firm.
Even in naivety, he is potent and virile.
He can whisper all day, knowing he won't lose his voice.
He is in perfect harmony with Nature and his own self-belief.
Possessing this harmony is displaying constancy.
Displaying constancy is displaying enlightenment.
Physical exuberance, he knows, is unwise.
Mental exhaustion, he knows, erodes capability.
What looks like strength will lead to stress.
This is contrary to Nature's Way.
That which opposes Nature's Way will soon perish.

The hunters knows that there is no creature who would attack man willingly. Thus he can walk field and wood without fear. Of course there are perils, though these can be avoided with experience and caution. He will avoid stepping on the sunning viper because he knows where the viper sleeps. He won't plunge his arm into the hornets nest, for knows which hole they employ. The Hunter is as vulnerable as any man yet in understanding Nature his trust in Her is implicit. Only feeling that he is part of Nature itself can allow this level of confidence. The Hunter is economic in his physical and mental effort. He knows that tiredness opposes balance. He understands that the weary mind cannot concentrate properly. All around him, Nature teaches steadiness and the value of respite. Witness the *modus operandi* of the high predators like the falcon or the leopard. The falcon rarely misses its prey. The leopard wears down its quarry. They spend hours simply watching, resting, building strength. The hunt, when the time is right, is a short period of extreme physical exertion and supreme mental focus. To hunt to over-exertion is common. To know when to rest is essential. To sit quietly and simply observe is a strength. To know when to move and to track down quarry must be the hunters forte. This is Natures Way. Therefore this is the Way of the Hunter.

Fifty Six

The wise talk seldom. They listen and watch.
Talking too much allows no time to become wise.
Seal the lips. Put up the barriers.
Temper the bitterness. Loosen the shoulders.
Extinguish the flame. Settle like dust.
This is primal retreat. This is retreat into Nature.
In this state, the wise achieve neutrality.
Ambivalent to friend, enemy, harm, favour, honour, disgrace.
They become the wild creature, who knows no such feelings.
This is absolute wisdom.

The real Hunter spends his time hunting, not talking about it. The proficient Hunter became so because when he wasn't hunting, he was learning about hunting. The wise are those who think they have never learned enough. The Hunter must resist argument and contention. He must act like his wild peers, they no such emotion as anger. The wild creatures rage of defence is nothing like the human capacity for simmering hatred or the bearing of a grudge. The Hunter must breathe deeply, close his mouth, unclench the fist, drop the shoulder, retire into quietness. The wise Hunter will seek the neutrality of the wild creature. It has no friend, therefore it has no enemy. It knows no fear, thus it cannot become anxious. It seeks no favour, therefore cannot feel inferior. It does not understand reputation, so disregards ignominy. This is how the Hunter should be.

Fifty Seven

Work the land with honesty and integrity.
Hunt with cunning and skill.
Minimise your impact on your environment.
Why is this the right Way? This is why.
Exerting pressure on your wild charges is negative.
They become suspicious and scared.
The wild creatures become sharp and alert.
They develop cunning and guile.
The more you entrap and restrain.
The more vulnerable they will become.
Other predators will arrive to attack them.
The wise Hunter works his land in rotation.
He allows restoration of numbers and confidence.
Undisturbed, wild things breed and strengthen.
Thus, not hunted, they lose fear and suspicion.

One of Natures biggest virtues is Her proclivity for maintaining balance. The Hunter needs to copy this trait. The competent farmer rotates his crops knowing that each will draw different nutrients or return fresh vitality to the land. The Hunter, the harvester of wild things, must apply the same balance to his acreage. The wise Hunter alternates his patrols and minimises pressure on quarry at any one place. Constant intimidation only serves to educate the wild creature and it will become wary and shrewd. The same also applies to trapping and snaring. Other predators learn where the regular snare is placed. The fox and the badger steal the rabbit before the Hunter completes his country rounds. The wily mink and the devious stoat raid the box-traps. The Hunter must learn to 'farm' his quarry and ensure future provision. There is no weakness in sparing the tiny rabbit kit, for it will grow to fit the cook-pot nicely and will breed before that time comes. The fair Hunter leaves the pigeon on Her nest, vulnerable though she seems. Beneath Her will lie double the yield if so allowed. Unless instructed, where pestilence threatens the land, the Hunter must learn to manage his potential harvest just like the farmer. Thus his quarry will live without stress and forget the stalkers intention. This is Natures Way.

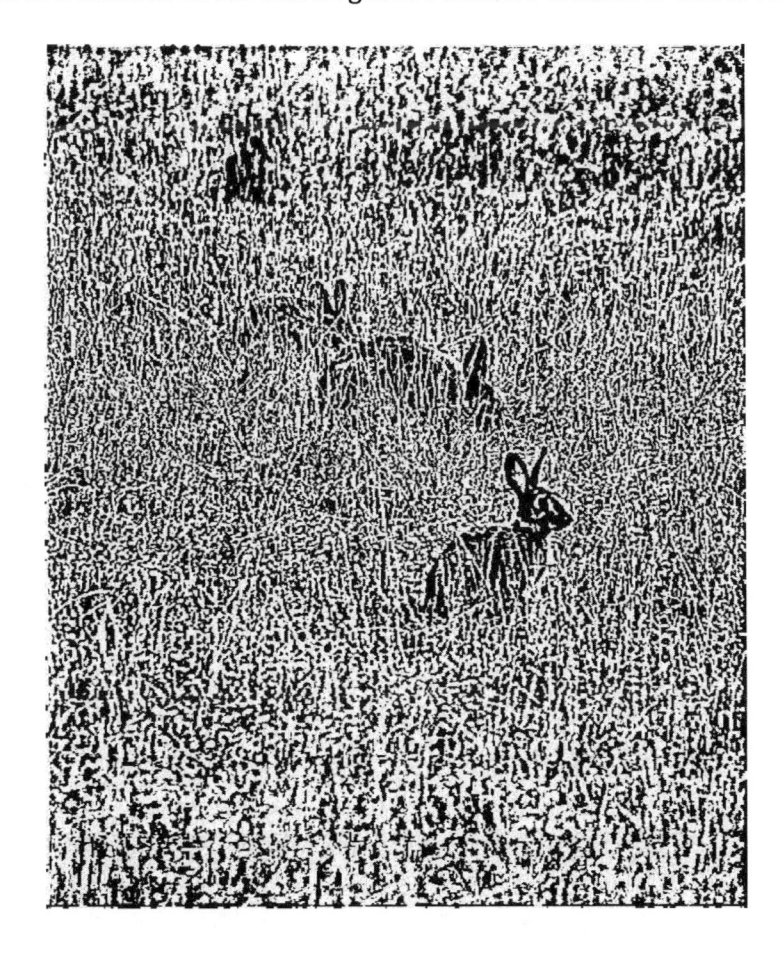

Fifty Eight

When the countryside is managed with a light hand.
Bird and beast exist simply and honestly.
When the land is hunted harshly, persistently.
The creatures become crafty and cunning.
In Nature, fortune often relies on misfortune.
Some things subdue for others to gain.
No creature knows when that time may come.
Nothing predetermines the outcome.
The cruel end might happen randomly, accidentally.
The efficient Way may appear, wrongly, the cruel Way.
This is an ancient dilemma.
The skilled Hunter is efficient and economical in dealing death.
He employs means which give fair law.
He acts compassionately, avoiding suffering.
He is knowledgeable, never condescending.

The Hunter who enjoys a large landscape on which to stalk will spread his attention widely, taking only a little from any area. Thus Nature will restore his crop and allow future harvest. Pogroms are undesirable, yet sometimes necessary. Where wild things cause disease or pollution and destroy crops or livestock to an unacceptable level then the Hunter must act. This is the hunters calling and Nature sanctions this. Nature herself promotes the principle of death being necessary to sustain life. The hierarchy that we call the 'food chain'? This is Natures design, it is part of the Way. Many folk, who fail to understand Nature, find confusion in this most simple of natural laws. Those that need to kill to feed are licensed by Nature to do so. There is no greater authority than Nature. All other authorities are surrogates. The endorsement is irrefutable. If the tiny robin can snatch up the wriggling caterpillar, then the sparrow-hawk may claim the robin for its supper. Life for life. If the Hunter catches the magpie at the black-caps nest, he stops the burglary. Life for life. The stoat rolls over a rabbit at the warren and sucks the blood from its neck. A slow and painful death, endorsed by Nature. The Hunter shoots the stoat, offering instant demise. Which Hunter was the most efficient? Nature knows.

Fifty Nine

In managing wildlife and serving Nature,
Conservation of species is paramount to the Hunter.
Thus conservation involves exercising restraint.
Restraint allows Nature to restore balance.
Balance maintains an abundance of Nature's bounty.
If we manage abundance, we are managing wisely.
And the principles of conservation will endure.
This is the deep rooted, firm foundation of Nature.
This is the Way of longevity and sustainability.

There is no credible Hunter who would seek obliteration of one of Natures species. The loss of any species at mankind's hand is an affront to Nature. The Hunter is part of Nature. Conservation is one of the hunters primary roles, yet misunderstood by many folk who wrongly see the Hunter as merely an assassin. There are few walking the earth who know the actual status of such species better than the Hunter, for he is in there, amongst Nature. The Hunter disregards censure, for it can only come from those who misunderstand Nature. Those who misunderstand Nature must be excused. The Hunter will follow Natures guidance and work to protect the defenceless and the vulnerable. He will cull the weak, harvest the abundant and protect the endangered.

Sixty

Managing wildlife is like preparing a rabbit for the pot.
Apply the simple principles which Nature employs.
Thus, the meal will not poison or corrupt.
Cut away the unsavoury, the unusable, the unhealthy.
Remove them in a Way which will not harm others.
Retain the prime, the succulent, the safe for the feast.
Serve up a meal that will sustain and refresh.

Part of the hunters role within Nature is to eradicate the weak, the diseased, the crop polluters, the spoilers, the raiders, the pirates, the bandits and the hijackers. The Hunter works to preserve the healthy and the robust so that its species endures and breeds to produce the most healthy offspring to ensure sustainability. In doing so, the Hunter also ensures the sustainability of his own harvest. Nature acts in the same Way. Sustaining the healthy and dispersing them to breed. Culling the weak through disease, hunger and predation, thus ensuring the survival and vigour of Her strongest charges.

Sixty One

The rolling countryside and the broad, flowing river.
These are the bed on which Nature reposes.
Laying like a maiden receptive to attention.
Maidens often use serenity to command a male.
Serenity appearing as subjugation and consent.
Therefore the stronger, in yielding to the weaker.
Often overcome the weaker.
And the weaker, in submitting to the stronger.
Conquer the stronger.
Can you see, then, that to overcome you must yield?
And that those who overcome, do so by yielding?
The strong desire control. The weak desire to serve.
For this to happen, in balance.
The strong must submit to the weak.

Nature's penchant for painting a canvas of vibrant colour and beauty belies the vast strength that she can wield. She is a brazen, beautiful temptress. Her splendour draws in the Hunter and entraps him. Once he has fallen for Natures charms he will never willingly abandon Her. Nature displays to the Hunter Her softness and vulnerability. She endows to the Hunter a position of dominance over many of Her charges. The foolish Hunter will think, therefore, that he is favoured by Nature. The wise Hunter knows well, however, that she is a fickle mistress and completely in control. The Hunter, learning from Nature, will employ the same tactic in many of his deeds and actions. The Way teaches how inaction can be more effective than action, how submission can achieve dominance, how subservience can create mastery. If the Hunter doubts this, he need only look to the hound at his side. The dog gains its place in the field with him through obedience and service yet becomes irreplaceable. The dog becomes at one with its master. The Hunter wants a hound he can control. The efficient hunting hound has an overwhelming desire to serve. Just as the Hunter wants to serve his mistress, Nature.

Sixty Two

Nature birthed the billion things.
She sustains the compassionate Hunter.
Yet she also feeds the cruel one.
The fair Hunter wins respect.
His methods are taught and admired.
These should be taught to the cruel Hunter.
The cruel Hunter loses land on which to hunt.
He becomes feared, despised, rejected.
Thus, even to the highest office.
The greatest treasure that is given.
Cannot be compared to this gift.
The teaching of existing at one with Nature.
Why did the ancients value this gift?
It has always been said that those who search will find.
The Hunter who finds will never go hungry.

A noted sage once said 'Give a man a fish and you will feed him for a day, teach him to fish and you will feed him for life'. This is one of the greatest gifts a man can give or receive. The knowledge of how to feed from forest, field, sea and stream. The Hunter, having acquired such valuable awareness, owes it to Nature to share it. The ethical Hunter, in passing on skills, passes on good practise and empathy. Nature will feed every Hunter, every fisherman, every gatherer and every trapper ... regardless of their method or agenda. The Hunter, however, in teaching these skills must encourage the student toward compassion and fair law. Cruelty and brutality are not the Hunters Way. It is the duty of the landowner and the companion to chastise the cruel Hunter, to try to set him on the correct path. The cruel Hunter brings prejudice and animosity to bear upon all hunters, from those who fail to understand hunting. In a world where more than half of the population cannot rely on being fed by its governance, hunting or farming or fishing or gathering is essential to survival. Knowing how to prepare the yield is crucial too. This is why the ancients held such worldly skills in such high esteem. To search, to find, to catch, to prepare, to cook, to serve, to feed. This is the Hunters Way.

Sixty Three

The good Hunter acts instinctively, yet respectfully.
He influences yet doesn't interfere.
He perceives the imperceptible and anticipates the unexpected.
Whether large, small, plentiful or rare, all is equal.
He ignores negativity and offers enlightenment.
He approaches each difficult task with a simple outlook.
He builds towards success with gradual steps, like Nature.
Nature makes huge achievement look effortless.
She makes complexity seem child's play.
The wise know their limitations and progress slowly.
Thus they achieve great success.
Promise, yet failure to deliver, breed mistrust.
Nature never fails to deliver.
Expect everything to be easy and you will struggle.
Nature never struggles. Nature takes it's time.
Yet all that Nature intends is achieved.
The seed that becomes the shoot, becomes the sapling.
The sapling becomes the tree that becomes the forest.
The wise confront difficulty and break it down.
In dismantling challenge, they never feel challenged.

The Hunter, hearing the *pipping* of the blackbird in the thicket, will anticipate the appearance of the fox. The sudden swerve of the flying wood-pigeon overhead tells the Hunter another human is abroad in the covert. The screech of the jay warns him of the approach of a grey squirrel, the jays mortal enemy. The panic of the hen pheasant and Her brood along the margin alerts the Hunter to the marauding stoat. The Hunter knows these things, for he has sat and watched them, or heard them, before. Thus, through experience, he anticipates much that few mortals would expect. Nature teaches the wise Hunter patience. He sees Her demonstrate incredible perseverance all the time. The gale topples the frail beech tree. The rain, sun and frosts soak and dry and crack the wood. The Hunter watches the slow decomposition of the fallen tree under a cloak of mycelium, which takes years to complete its feast. Nature breaks down the task using successive steps, at the same time replacing the tree. The Hunter watches the beech mast seed and climb, over his lifetime, towards the woods canopy. The Hunter sees the fragility of both the common and the rare. One becomes the other, then Nature rolls the dice again. The grey squirrel usurps the red squirrel and all men turn a hand against the grey. The rabbit population rises and falls like an ocean swell. The wise man learns to follow Natures example. The challenging undertaking is broken down into manageable tasks and each is accomplished in turn. The wise man will never feel pressure. He will say that it will be done when it is finished, not before. That is how Nature has taught him. *In Nature, nothing hurries, yet everything is accomplished.*

Sixty Four

Harmony, with diligence, is simple to maintain.
Tackle the strangle-weed while it is fragile.
Slay it before it can outgrow control.
Where possible, prevent it before it can germinate.
Deal with it before it gains a foothold.
The pine tree large enough to throw your arms around ?
It started as a cone, then small shoot, then tender sapling.
The tower stretching to three storeys ?
It began as a scraped pile of earth.
The journey of a thousand miles ?
It started with that first single step.
Many fall at the last hurdle, just missing success.
Plan to reach the end, as you planned the start.
Then you will clear the final hurdle.
The Hunter refrains from the unnecessary.
He hunts the tangible, he does not chase shadows.
He learns by failing and thus educates through experience.
He undoes the false conservation of the misinformed.
He helps restore the balance of the billion things.
And he achieves this within the principles of Nature.

Nature does not judge between the right and the wrong of a living things existence. She does not interfere when the weed stifles the flower, when the insect infests the crop or when vermin plunder the grain. It is our prerogative, as one of Natures living things, to cut down the weed, to destroy the infestation and to cull the pest. As with all deeds, to act little and often is more effective than waiting until a problem is out of control. The Hunter plans his actions to be measured and incremental. To plan with a view on how to finish is wise, yet to actually start is the wisest thing of all. Without roots, the lofty pine would topple over. Without firm foundations, the brick tower would sink. Thus we are taught that high aspiration needs solid basis. Start strong and you will finish strong. Fail to plan and you will fail to accomplish. Set forth and you can strive. Procrastinate and you will never set out. The Hunter, in his very demeanour, should be a pragmatist. He lives in a colourful world but sees everything in black and white. Every success is taken with gratitude. Every failure is merely a lesson. Each step is unhurried yet focused. He wastes no breath and strains no muscle. Like Nature, he flows from plan to purpose. His knowledge of life and the living, of death and the delivery, sanction him to act as judge, jury and executioner in the restoration of natural balance. Nature herself permits this and there is no greater arbiter than Nature. If the Hunter would dare to dress in the mantle of the adjudicator, he must also wear the badges of morality and restraint. The Hunter should exhibit an affinity with the wild and with wild things which mirrors the behaviour of Nature herself. Impartial but governing. Tolerant but assertive.

Sixty Five

Those that first explored Nature chose not to share Her wisdom.
They used it to subjugate, not educate.
But this domination was soon usurped by the wise.
For the wise realised that Nature was a common treasure.
The gift of Nature to mankind was a blessing.
Free access to Nature's wilderness is a primal right.
She transcends power and precedes knowledge.
Her freedom is profound, thus she releases everyone's spirit.

There came a time in man-kinds past where the wise and the ancient were overtaken by the demand for industry and profit. A time when the rural became the urban and where many men took to service rather than independence. The artisan skills of the Hunter gatherer were lost to all but a few. Possession of land became more important than the wild creatures or the people within it. Enclosure and enactment sought to exclude the access of man and beast. In time, man-kinds own wisdom has over-turned such folly and slowly access to land is returned to those who seek to watch Nature at Her work. Nature rewards such study and affinity with unparalleled drama, beauty and phenomena.

Sixty Six

Notice how the ocean enjoys higher status than the river or stream.
It lies lower than them, they flow down into the oceans vastness.
Thus, the ocean, without touching them.
Sustains a billion fertile valleys and watercourses.
For the Hunter to become successful.
He must lie low like the ocean, let everything flow to him.
He must treat Nature's creatures with humility.
For the Hunter to lead, he must stand behind.
To dominate, he must be below.
This Way, nothing feels oppressed.
The Hunter's presence will not cause fear and alarm.
Nature will accept him, she will not tire of him.
And because he does not compete, he has no competition.

Nature constantly demonstrates to the Hunter the importance of inaction to attainment. The principle of withdrawal in order to achieve success. Of sitting low to reach high. The Hunter thus learns to weigh up his options and to act like Nature herself. He will see the futility of chasing the coney. Why not sit and wait for the coney to come to him? He will know where it feeds. He will sit in the shadows and wait. Nor will he act as soon as he sees his quarry. He will study it a while. He will wait until many of his quarry are feeding close to him. He knows that if two coneys are feeding and one expires, the other will know and remember. If thirty coneys are feeding and one expires, the others will ignore the incident. Thus, with no pressure felt, he can take another. And perhaps another, but he will judge when to stop. Can you see, therefore, how in restraint comes conquest? With patience, comes reward? Just like the vast ocean, the Hunter sits low and holds power. If he lets everything flow to him, taking without interfering. The sea will rarely disturb the valley or ravine that feeds it. It takes from, and thus sustains, the valley.

Sixty Seven

All of mankind should understand the wonder of Nature.
This wonder puts Nature beyond compare.
If she could be compared to anything, she would not be Nature.
The Hunter must hold three treasures close to his heart.
The first is compassion. Some call this mercy.
The second is conservation. Some call this husbandry.
The third is humility. Before Nature, we are nothing.
Compassion enables merciful action and banishes cruelty.
Conservation encourages generosity and thrift.
Humility promotes respect, the cornerstone of leadership.
To have action without compassion ?
To be generous without conserving ?
To lead without humility ?
These are all recipes for disaster.
Hunt with compassion and you will hunt well.
Conserve and the reward will be sustainability.
This is how Nature's behaves. With humility.

The Hunter must remember that the bearing of arms which can dominate even the strongest of beasts is a responsibility to bear solemnly. Nature will look harshly at the man who abuses such power. The judicious Hunter takes no life without absolute and clear purpose, be it for food, crop preservation, health protection or husbandry. To be merciful need not mean abstinence but means simply showing efficiency and swiftness. A quick death is not a cruel death. The python slowly crushes its victim, yet is not called cruel? It kills in the only proficient Way it knows. The Hunter, too, must be proficient. Conservation is a much maligned concept. The Hunter knows that conservation doesn't mean keeping everything alive. It means not destroying all of a species. These are two very different interpretations. Often the Hunter culls to conserve, strengthening the wild stock and weeding out disease or mutation. The essence of conservation is knowing when and where to act. More importantly, when to withdraw and suspend activity. This is why the Hunter and his peers impose self-regulation and seasons, to allow breeding and restoration of the warren, the herd and the flock. Few will understand that the Hunter can behave with compassion and conservatism. They see only the death he brings, not the veneration for life that he holds. Why would the Hunter seek to destroy all that he hunts? That would be madness. Nature understands this.

Sixty Eight

The competent Hunter is never cruel.
The skilled predator doesn't act with malice.
The blackbird bears no guilt over the worm.
The sparrow-hawk strikes without conscience.
The successful stalker does not gloat.
He acts, always, with humility.
This is the virtue of compassion.
Thus he moves, within Nature, respected by Nature.
Achieving this displays true, ancient harmony with Nature.

To the apprentice Hunter, to cause death often either disturbs or excites. Neither reaction is wrong, if it brings reflection. Neither reaction is wrong, if there was no hatred involved. Trust me when I say that for the experienced Hunter, the death itself never excites but the stalk that led to it is what makes the heart race and the blood course. In the compassionate Hunter, you will see pity. In the most efficient Hunter, you will see modesty. In the balanced Hunter, you will see humility. To know how to hunt takes a lifetime of learning. To spend ones lifetime hunting is an honour. Nature bestows this honour. Nature therefore respects the Hunter and the Hunter respects Nature. Moving within Nature, valuing Nature, being valued by Nature. That is the Hunter's Way.

Sixty Nine

The ancient warriors used to have a saying:
I dare not be the host and would rather be the guest.
I would rather withdraw a full pace than advance an inch.
To the Hunter, this means moving without showing malice.
It means being ready to strike without appearing tense.
Like the kestrel watching voles in the grass.
It means reaching prey without them sensing predation.
Like the ghosting owl, hunting with stealth.
It means using guile, not showing malice.
There is no greater folly than under-estimating your prey.
In doing so, you will return empty handed.
Thus when Hunter meets his quarry, the calmest will prevail.

There is much truth in the ancient philosophies. The Hunter, as a visitor to the forest, can enjoy its hospitality far more than the forester or woodman. His purpose is not to tend the root and tree, thus he can spend much time in quiet vigil. The hunters retires into the shadows rather than stepping into sight. Invisible and inactive, he achieves. Self discipline, stealth, restraint, patience ... these are the Hunter's Way. Watch how the vixen prowls towards the rabbits, stopping often, measuring their demeanour. Study the humble frog as it sits immobile, surrounded by flies. The strike of the unfurling tongue is deadly accurate, yet unexpected. Witness the barn owls noiseless hunt. The almost imperceptible squeak of fright from the vole is what gives away its position. Thus serenity overcomes anxiety. A valuable lesson from Nature. The wise Hunter seeks success without exposure and retreat with anonymity. He was there but he was never there. Like Nature. This is the wisdom that the ancients taught. Insignificance triumphs.

Seventy

All that I am writing is proven and understandable.
Yet few men attain this level of unity with Nature.
These are ancient words, based in reality.
Nature's own principles underpin them.
If the Hunter does not truly understand Nature.
They will not understand these words.
The few that are enlightened and follow Nature's Way?
Their larders are full and they are nourished by Nature.
Though they appear humble, they are rich beyond measure.

The Hunter, the forester and the farmer ... who work within Nature with no bias .. can expect to achieve an understanding and knowledge of Nature that surpasses many other of Her casual visitors. The naturalist and the conservationist, though they may love wild flora and fauna, can lean towards conflict with Nature. Nature allows both life and death yet some choose to dismiss this most basic of natural principles. For all ... Hunter, farmer, forester, naturalist and conservationist ... good intention and co-operation serve Nature best. Let the Hunter hunt. Let the forester fell. Let the farmer plough. Let the naturalist study. Let the conservationist strive to protect. Let Nature decide which is right or wrong. If each feels passionately that they are right, then all is well in Nature.

Seventy One

The Hunter who recognises he has much to learn.
That is the most accomplished Hunter.
Be like the grey heron, a skilful predator.
Always watchful, studying the landscape.
Be like the fox, eternally curious.
The Hunter who thinks he already knows it all.
Will never be the most skilled Hunter.
Knowledge must be continually attained.
Attainment only comes with recognition of need to learn.
The wise Hunter is faultless.
Because he recognises he has faults.
So he repairs them, thus becomes faultless.

The pursuit of knowledge is perpetual for every man, particularly the Hunter. A wise man once said 'Live as though you will die tomorrow but learn as though you will live forever'. The Hunter who states that he knows it all will become the weakest Hunter. The Hunter who craves knowledge with every breath will hold his esteem as the wisest of hunters. This principle is true for every man or woman, in every pursuit. Curiosity is the source of sagacity. Observation is the conduit for understanding. The Hunter learns best by watching the beast and bird. They have acute vision, advanced hearing and a keen sense of smell. Superior to the Hunter in all aspects. Yet the Hunter has the far greater advantage in watching this behaviour of understanding, remembering and reasoning. The astute Hunter will always notice that which he never registered before and will memorise it. The new track, the fresh scent, the different behaviour. Thus the Hunter, in recognising his own naivety, grows ever more knowledgeable.

Seventy Two

When the people lose respect for Nature.
They will bring to bear their own destruction.
This is why Nature does not interfere with their actions.
This is why Nature does not interrupt their industry.
Nature's Way is not direct interference.
Nature allows the billion things to intervene for Her.
That is why the people should respect Nature.
The Hunter, therefore, watches without interfering.
He has self-respect but not arrogance.
He discards loftiness and chooses humility.

The Hunter moves in a world of contradiction. Those who question his Way of life and methods are those most responsible for the destruction and abomination of the wild. They see Nature as a goldfish bowl, superfluous to their daily existence and something to be enjoyed when it takes their fancy. They fail to see that Nature will endure long after their institutions, their false temples and their arrogance has evaporated. The Hunter trusts that Nature will ultimately persevere and therefore chooses Her company over the shallow and the materialistic. The Hunter rejects criticism unless it comes from Nature herself. He enjoys the humility of understanding what others of his own species will never appreciate. That they exist only because Nature permits them to. The plague, the tsunami, the earthquake, the flood and the famine confirm the hunters wisdom.

Seventy Three

The bold and reckless creature may be killed.
The brave yet cunning creature may survive.
Which deserve which? Who knows?
Nature has favoured one but not the other.
Only Nature herself knows why.
Nature doesn't wrestle, yet she asserts.
She says nothing but has all the answers.
She cannot be summoned, yet she arrives.
Nature does not hurry, yet all is achieved.
She casts Her coarse-meshed net wide.
Yet nothing evades Her.

Nature is a fair maiden but a fickle mistress. She displays beauty and allure with little abandon yet no living thing enjoys immunity from Her ambiguity. Some thrive, some fail. Some live, some die. Strength can dissolve to weakness, frailty can emerge as power. Such is Natures capriciousness. The Hunter never questions this. What Nature desires, Nature attains. What Nature allows will happen, that which she vetoes will not. No man can question this, Nature allows no tribunal. The Hunter understands this and accepts Natures judgement. The Hunter knows one thing for certain, which many folk fail to appreciate. Nothing escapes Natures attention. She is everywhere, always. Anything that lives is within Her accountability ... therefore everything that breeds, grows, feeds, ails and dies is Her responsibility too. The wise Hunter understands this and acts accordingly, respecting Nature and Her charges. Disrespect life and you disrespect Nature.

Seventy Four

Nature's billion things do not fear death.
So they cannot be threatened with death.
The wild creature cannot anticipate dying.
Only mankind lives in constant fear of dying.
Such that the law often threatens death as retribution.
Threatened with death, who would break the law?
The wild creature abides by Nature's laws, not man-kinds.
Thus the buzzard doesn't avoid the pheasant pen.
If we set rules that are un-Natural.
We must expect Nature's creatures to break them.

The wild animal and bird recognises threat and senses menace, yet it is not within its capability to foresee death. Not expecting death it cannot fear death. Only man is foolish enough to waste his life worrying about when death will come and what lies beyond it. The wise know this is improvident. Life is to be lived now and to expect anything beyond this life is pure conceit. Thus, like his wild counterpart, the Hunter walks the forest in denial of death. The Hunter also understands how the wild creature, not fearing death, will act with disdain for the false edicts and irrelevant decrees of mankind. These are not Natures laws so don't concern the animal or bird. We can throw a pen around the pheasant poults to hold off the fox but to the buzzard, the barrier means nothing. It will swoop in to feed, without fear. For that is the Hunter's Way.

Seventy Five

Harvest too much from field and wood.
And all the wild creatures will starve.
If wild creatures are starved from their own territory.
They will raid the hen-house and the granary.
Why does the fox risk the hen-house?
Why does the hawk plunder the pheasant poults?
Because they must feed or die.
Death holds no fear for those who would die anyway.

The veteran Hunter knows how to farm his territory carefully and ensure not just ample yield but also frugality. He knows that putting his quarry under pressure will not help to sustain a future harvest. This applies to prey species too. If the Hunter removes too much of the staple prey in the food chain, he will drive the higher predators toward the flock and the farm. They too must eat and who can blame them plundering the livestock, the granary and the poultry if man himself has taken away their natural food source? The starving creature will not hold conscience nor fear man when its needs to find food. To feed and to drink are basic rights within Nature and the Way.

Seventy Six

The living being is tender and pliant.
The corpse is rigid and stiff.
The willow wand is soft and supple in life.
Yet it is tough and brittle in death.
Thus the unyielding Hunter is following death.
The flexible Hunter is following life.
The rigid shooter will miss his target.
Only the relaxed Hunter will succeed.
The hard and the cruel occupy a low status.
The compassionate and controlled take the higher ground.

Just as Nature teaches us how inaction can be more effective than action, she also shows us that to survive and live long, we must remain flexible and pliant. Not just in body but also in mind. Not just in deed but also in thought. The relaxed sinew and the gentle breath hold the eye steadily on the crosshair. Tension and rigidity spoil the aim. Kindness and compassion are valuable additions to the hunters toolbox. They engender trust and respect. Cruelty and brutality are the Way of the ruffian. They are not the Hunter's Way. The brutal and the hard see only death therefore they follow death. The kind and the sympathetic see the life as more important than the death therefore they are following life. Those that follow life are following Nature. Those that follow life are following the Way. Those that follow the Way enjoy a fruitful and full life themselves.

Seventy Seven

Nature's action resembles the drawing of an archers bow.
As the string is drawn, the high point is lowered.
At the same time the low point is raised.
If the string is too slack, it is shortened.
If the string is too tight, it is lengthened.
Thus Nature's balance acts like the bow.
She lowers the high, raises the low.
The roebuck looks drab, while the dragonfly is handsome.
She reduces excess and compensates dearth.
The gale fells the timber and the lowly will feast.
Sadly, mankind often opposes Nature.
It takes from the needy and gives to the wealthy.
But there is a gift that should be shared with all.
Needy or wealthy. That is the gift of knowledge.
The wise share knowledge without conceit,
Without taking credit and without claiming status.

The Hunter is privileged to see Natures constant balancing action. He feels the rain that hydrates the planted seed. He tastes the breeze that spreads the fertile pollen. He notes the blight that corrupts the crop and the disease that levels the crowded warren. Where there is drought she brings water. Where there is famine she provides food. Nature is like the drawing of the hunters slingshot. The pull in one direction delivers propulsion in the other. This is what Nature does. She often dresses the low creature in high colour and the high creature in plain hue. The jay is gaudy yet the buzzard is drab. The most beautiful birds have the harshest song. Listen to the peacock or the goldfinch. The dullest birds have the most melodic song. Listen to the warbler or the skylark. Often the high predator is distinct and its prey is dowdy, thus giving protection to the prey. Look at the tiger or the leopard then see the antelope or the springbok. This is how Nature achieves equilibrium. She distributes Her gifts and Her privilege evenly. The greatest of Her gifts she bestows on man. The gift of Her wisdom and the ability to share it. If the Hunter pulls from Nature he owes it to Her to push Her knowledge. Thus the wise Hunter shares his wisdom freely. He will tutor and mentor not only the methods and manner of hunting but also the behaviour, the habit and the habitat of bird and beast.

Seventy Eight

Water is one of Nature's softest elements.
Yet nothing can stand in its path indefinitely.
There is no other element to match it.
The soft, with persistence, can erode the hard.
Nature shows us this with water.
Yet, though we can see this plainly,
Few understand this simple, Natural law.
The Hunter should understand this law.
Act humbly before Nature and she will embrace you.
Move softly, fluidly, among the billion things.
You will slip between them like a brook finding its course.
Strange as it seems, this is the truth.

The great ravines, chasms, caves and valleys that cover the earth were all carved over eons by water, or Her solid entity, ice. The gentle, persistent action of one of the softest elements erodes all beneath it as it powers its Way relentlessly towards the ocean. On its Way it changes everything that it touches. It travels using the paths of least resistance yet will not be hindered. It will progress sometimes gently, at others with force. This is also Natures Way. Water follows Natures model. So too should the Hunter. He should move with intent and with purpose. Gently and gracefully. Determined if opposed yet flexible if diverted. The Hunter, moving through the forest will do so a few steps at a time, stopping to weigh up his options. Like the trickle of the exploring brook, he will look for the route which offers the fastest progress and the least opposition. Thus the stream finds the river and the river finds the ocean. Thus the Hunter finds his trail and the trails leads to his quarry. The Hunter's Way follows Natures Way.

Seventy Nine

Following one of Nature's great events, such as a great flood,
There may be flotsam, jetsam, famine and plague.
The cynical will cry "What has Nature done to us"?
The wise however understand that Nature had purpose.
They will not demand that Nature redresses the balance.
Nature owns the contract. It is for us to balance the books.
Nature is impartial. She cannot be wrong.

Many folk only learn to respect Nature when she displays unexpected fury. The torrent, the tsunami, the hurricane, the typhoon, the lightning bolt, the drought, the famine. Why did they happen? The answer is simple. Because Nature deigned they must happen to level Her purpose. They are a consequence, not the act. If the act was to throw water onto the land, then the torrent is merely consequence. If the earthquake settled the earths surface, the tsunami is merely consequence. Nature doesn't care that man is in its Way, any more so than bird or beast or fish. She is independent.

Eighty

The wise Hunter avoids crowds and works quietly, alone.
He possesses enough equipment to do the work.
He knows his craft intimately and needs few devices.
He labours locally, harvesting familiar land.
He will have traps and decoys and nets.
Yet he will rarely need to use them.
He may have an array of guns, slingshots and blades.
Yet he will never display them or brag of them.
Would that everyone led this simple life, close to Nature?
Savouring the food they hunt, content with simple clothing.
Happy in their homes. Satisfied with their lives.
Shunning materialism. Ignoring their neighbours status.
Leaving others to live as they choose to live.
Would that everyone could exist in such harmony?

The Hunter will always attempt to employ tactic over implements, cunning over devices, yet he may possess many contraptions. These will only be used when all else fails for the wise Hunter prefers to travel lightly and unburdened. He will work enough land to keep him busy yet not too much for him to cover economically. His territory will be intimately known to him. So too will be its flora and fauna. He will know every ditch, every dyke, every spinney, every crop, every meadow, every brook and every pond. He will mark all tracks and trails. He will know where the hare passes through hedge, where the deer leaps the wire and where the rabbit slips under the gate. The best Hunter will always be the one who uses one rifle or one bow or one slingshot. For he will know how to use it almost with his eyes closed. Just as the fox needs only cunning, teeth and paws so the hunters should need only field-craft and his choice of tool. The Hunter will exist simply, satisfied with his status within Nature, content with home and family, coveting nothing. The Hunter will know he is a lucky man, rich in knowledge, under pressure from no-one.

Eighty One

The words that people need to hear.
Rarely fall well on the ear.
They are harsh like the jackdaws shout.
The wise don't argue or seek conflict.
Those that argue are not wise.
Those who think they know everything, know little.
The wise are those who claim never to know enough.
Constantly seeking knowledge and wisdom.
The wise don't worry about accumulating wealth.
They gain spiritual affluence through helping others.
The more they give, the richer they feel.
Nature's Way is to balance, not to destroy.
Nature's Way is to assist, not to oppose.

The Hunter seeks to work through life without conflict. Those who misunderstand his purpose or his methods are better avoided than confronted. There are none so deaf as those who will not hear. There are none so blind as those who will not see. To argue, even if you believe you are right, is wasteful. When two bulls go head to head there is little concession and even less progression. Those who claim they know rarely do. Those who are open to learning are more likely to be wise. Withdraw from debate and profit from progress. The Hunter, understanding the finality of death, must spend his life in positive pursuit. Argument, conflict, combat? These contradict Nature. Harmony, respect, philosophy? These are Natures Way, therefore they are the Hunter's Way. The Hunter, in not seeking prosperity, will become wealthy in spirit. He can have no enemy if he chooses not to fight. He will be part of Nature if he chooses Natures path. He will be wise if he chooses to learn. He will be respected if he acts with compassion. He will be remembered if he chooses to teach. Choose the Hunter's Way. Choose life, now.

Reflections on the '"Tao Te Ching"'

I would never have embarked on this project if the original transcript of the 'Tao Te Ching' hadn't had a profound effect on my day to day thinking. Throughout my adult life I have followed motivational writers and speakers, appreciating the little push that a piece of shared wisdom can supply. As the increasing trickle of platitudes attributed to Lao Tzu increased, I decided to turn on the tap and find out who this guy was and what he was about?

When I read the '"Tao Te Ching"' the penny dropped very quickly. It was funny to reflect that the pressures we endure today and consider to be afflictions of modern living were actually no different to life two thousand and six hundred years ago! So, what did I learn that has influenced my life and how am I applying it? There are several simple concepts, all reflected here in The Hunter's Way, which are absolute life-changers.

The '"Tao Te Ching"' teaches that inaction is as powerful as action. As a Hunter, you would already appreciate that. You sit quietly in cover and the action comes to you. You control your emotions, your breathing and make a judgement before reacting. You hold the power. Do you do that in the day job? I didn't used to. Try it. It works. You get that 'controlling' or 'nasty' e-mail from a boss or colleague. You used to bite back, e-mail wars! Just ignore it. See what happens. They have been relying on you to feed their 'psychoses'. Now they're dying of hunger so they pick another victim. When they come back to you it will be because they need you. You have the control back. The customer who wants to complain about your service, unfairly, just to get the bill reduced? Withdraw the service. Hit them with inaction, not reaction. The meeting room, the board room .. everyone throwing you bait because you usually bite and ignite? Avoid eye contact, study some papers, don't get drawn. Inaction. The room will fall silent and if you were to look up, everyone would be staring at you. You hold the power. Use it as you choose. Someone throws you an unachievable deadline. Ignore it. Inaction.

Remember .. 'In Nature, nothing hurries, yet everything is achieved'.

The Way concept of nothingness often having greater value than substance is fascinating. The hollow hub of a wheel is so important. Without it, the axle can't fit, so the wheel is useless. The cooking vessel? If there were no space within you couldn't put food in to cook. The space is nothingness. But it gives the vessel its functionality. Think about this in 'life' terms. The love of a partner, a child, a pet. It is intangible but can physically affect you and motivate you. The
aroma of a favourite meal. Intangible but powerful. The sound of your favourite band. Personally, I can't write fluently without a soundtrack in the background. I can't grab music or hold it but, boy, does it inspire me. My last book was written on the back of a Kings Of Leon soundtrack. This one ? Joe Bonamassa, live.

The biggest statement in the Tao which has taught to me slow down and exorcise stress from my life related to that statement above. That Nature never hurries yet everything is accomplished. I don't do deadlines anymore, in work or in writing. Deadlines are someone else's agenda, someone else's stress. Anything I do now is only ready when it's finished, when I'm happy with the finished product. Which is quite amazing in itself. I just wrote this book and processed the pics, with no deadline, in eight weeks. Because it was my own agenda, no-one else's. Because I have a day job and enjoy writing for a couple of hours every night, that means I wrote this book in about 100 hours. When people have been relying on your punctuality they ignore the stress you've been under to deliver. Don't deliver on time, always. Be late! People panic, then your delivery is respected more.

There is one popular piece of wisdom regularly attributed to Lao Tzu which influenced my life recently, yet I can find no reference to this in the '*"Tao Te Ching"*' or any other of his writings. It is this:

'If you are depressed, you are living in the past. If you are anxious, you are living in the future. To achieve inner peace, you must live in the present'.

I have no idea who really authored this, but it is a supremely powerful concept. I used to wake in the middle of the night and start to worry. Did I do enough today and what have I got to do tomorrow? Now, I lie back and reflect on that concept. I switch into 'now' and listen to the tawny owl hooting outside or the hum of the ceiling fan, maybe my lovely wife snoring lightly? And I think .. you lucky, lucky man. It doesn't take long to drift off to sleep again. Stuck in a traffic jam, I look around for things I've never seen before because I've driven past them. I keep a camera on the passenger seat and look for photo opportunities. Some days, I pray for traffic jams!

Acknowledgements

There are many, many interpretations of the *'Tao Te Ching'* so trying to find a reliable original translation can be difficult. Many authors have done exactly as I have just done. They have added distortion to the original text to meet their own agenda. Thus I am indebted to Derek Lin for his translation at www.Taoism.net and his *'Tao Te Ching'*: Annotated & Explained', published by Skylight Paths in 2006. This work gave me the 'ground-zero' from which to build my own interpretation.

I am indebted also to the following couple who freely supplied the only image in this book not photographed by me personally:

Steve and Hayley Long for the picture of the cartwheel in Chapter Eleven.

About The Author

Ian Barnett is a freelance country sports and hunting journalist based in Norfolk, UK. Ian has hunted with airguns and lurchers since his teens and writes regularly for the airgun press about hunting fieldcraft. He is also a keen wildlife and landscape photographer. Many of Ian's images can be seen on his Wildscribbler website:

http://ianbarnett18.wix.com/wildscribbler

As well as many hundreds of magazine articles, Ian has several published books to his credit. There is a website dedicated to this particular book and which links to all Ian's other books. Ian also writes a regular blog on the website:

http://www.thehuntersway.co.uk/

Printed in Great Britain
by Amazon.co.uk, Ltd.,
Marston Gate.